Redefining Literacy 2.0

SECOND EDITION

David F. Warlick

Linworth
Books

Professional Development Resources for
K-12 Library Media and Technology Specialists

Library of Congress Cataloging-in-Publication Data

Warlick, David F.
  Redefining literacy 2.0 / David F. Warlick. -- 2nd ed.
     p. cm.
  Redefining literacy two point zero
  Redefining literacy two point oh
  Revised version of the author's: Redefining literacy for the 21st century.
  Includes bibliographical references.
  ISBN-13: 978-1-58683-333-6 (pbk.)
  ISBN-10: 1-58683-333-2 (pbk.)
  1. Computers and literacy. 2. Education--Effect of technological innovations on. 3. Curriculum planning. I. Warlick, David F. Redefining literacy for the 21st century. II. Title. III. Title: Redefining literacy two point zero. IV. Title: Redefining literacy two point oh.
  LC149.5.W35 2008
  371.33'4--dc22
                              2008034191

Cynthia Anderson: Editor
Judi Repman: Consulting Editor

Published by Linworth Publishing, Inc.
3650 Olentangy River Road
Suite 250
Columbus, Ohio 43214

ISBN 13: 978-1-58683-333-6
ISBN 10: 1-58683-333-2

Mixed Sources
Product group from well-managed forests and other controlled sources
www.fsc.org Cert no. SW-COC-002283
© 1996 Forest Stewardship Council

5 4 3 2

Table of Contents

Table of Figures vi
Acknowledgments viii
About the Author viii
Introduction ix
    User's Guide xiii

Chapter 1: A Day in the Life of School 2.0—2015 1
    The Story 1
    Assumptions About the Future 5
    Assumptions—New Tools 7
    Assumptions—How the Information Flows 9
    Assumptions—What We Do with New Tools .11
    Assumptions—Curriculum and the New Tools 12
    Critical Question for Educators and Communities 14

Chapter 2: Exposing What Is True 15
    A Brief History of Networked Digital Information 18
    Finding the Information—Hypertext Environments 22
    Investigative Strategies—Personal Digital Libraries 25
    Investigative Strategies—Finding Witnesses .29
        Community 29
        Mailing Lists 30
        The Blogosphere 33
    Investigative Strategies—Finding Evidence 35
    Investigative Strategies—Search Logs 40
    Investigative Strategies—Search Language 41
    Search Tools 43
    Investigative Strategies—RSS (Training the Information to
      Find You) 44
        How RSS Works 45
    Investigative Strategy—Evaluating the Information 49
        Gatekeeping as a Literary Skill 50
        Have you heard of this? 52
        Does this make sense? 52
        Who is the source? 53
        Does the domain seem legitimate? 53
        Who owns the domain? 54
        What else does the site offer? 54
    Investigative Strategy—More Questions 56
        Literacy Invoking Assignment 56
        Who? 57
        What? 57
        When? 58

Where? 58
Investigative Strategy—Defend Your Information 60
Conclusion 61
Action Items 61
Directors of Technology 61
Principals and Head Teachers 62
Media Specialists 63
School Tech Facilitators 63
Teachers 64
Students 64
Parents 64

Chapter 3: Employing the Information 67
Capacity for Information 68
Product to Process 69
Issues of Intellectual Property 70
Indexed Content 70
Working Tabular Data 74
Employing Text 69
Employing Web Content–Advanced 76
Employing Images 77
Mixing Visuals 77
Employing Audio 81
Employing Audio with Podcasting 83
Employing Video 85
Sources for Images to Employ 86
Sources for Audio to Employ 87
Sources for Video to Employ 88
Employing RSS Feeds 89
Employing the Web (Mashups) 90
Web Mashups 93
Machinima 94
Conclusion 94
Action Items 96
Directors of Technology 96
Principals 96
Media Specialists 97
School Tech Facilitators 98
Teachers 98
Students 99
Parents 99

Chapter 4: Expressing Ideas Compellingly 101
Communicating Compellingly—Text 102
Expressing Text Compellingly 106

New Opportunities for Expressing Text 109

    Blogging 109

    Wikis and Other Collaborative Writing Tools 110

Communicating Compellingly—Images 112

    Teachers and Images 113

    Students and Images 113

Communicating Compellingly—Animation .116

    Flash 117

    GIF Animations 117

    Video Animation 118

    Presentations as Animation 119

Communicating Compellingly—Video Production 120

Communicating Compellingly—Web Publishing 124

Some Technical Aspects 125

Facilitating School or Classroom Web Sites 126

Planning 128

Programming as a Communication Skill 129

    Opportunities for Students to Program Computers 130

Conclusion 131

Action Items 132

    Directors of Technology 132

    Principals and Head Teachers 133

    Media Specialists 133

    School Tech Facilitators 134

    Teachers 134

    Students 135

    Parents 135

Chapter 5: Ethics and Context 137

Ethics and the Age of Information 137

Information as Property 138

    Creative Commons 142

Information Reliability 145

Information Infrastructure 147

A Student and Teacher Code of Ethics 151

    A Student and Teachers Information Code of Ethics 151

Cybersafety 153

Action Items 155

    Directors of Technology 155

    Principals and Head Teachers 156

    Media Specialists 156

    School Tech Facilitators 156

    Teachers 157

    Students 157

    Parents 157

Chapter 6: Implementation 159
    1. Learning in the New Information Landscape 161
    2. Learning within New Conversations 162
    3. Modeling the Learning Lifestyle 163
    Personal Learning Networks 164
        Tips for Cultivating Your Personal Learning Network 167
        Tips for Pruning Your Personal Learning Network 168
    Action Items 170
        Directors of Technology 170
        Principals 171
        Media Specialists 171
        School Tech Facilitators 171
        Teachers 172
        Students 172
        Parents 172

Chapter 7: Conclusion 173
    Becoming Resourceful Learners 173

Appendix A • Other Suggested Works—Books .176
Appendix B • Other Suggested Works—Web Documents 177
Appendix C • Where to Find the Future 178
Appendix D • Creative Commons Designations 178
Works Cited 179

Table of Figures

Figure 0.1:   Converging Conditions xiii
Figure 1.1:   Virtual Presentation 10
Figure 1.2:   3E Literacy 14
Figure 2.1:   3-Dimensional Reading 22
Figure 2.2:   Hyperlinks 25
Figure 2.3:   Bookmarks 26
Figure 2.4:   Volunteer Form 30
Figure 2.5:   Mailing Lists 31
Figure 2.6:   E-Mail 33
Figure 2.7:   Search 39
Figure 2.8:   Search Cycle 40
Figure 2.9:   Search Evaluation 41
Figure 2.10: HTML-RSS 43
Figure 2.11: RSS Buttons 46
Figure 2.12: Aggregator Layout 47

Figure 2.13:   Start Page Layout 48
Figure 2.14:   Digital Index Card 59
Figure 3.1:   BlogPulse 1 71
Figure 3.2:   BlogPulse 2 72
Figure 3.3:   Tag Cloud 72
Figure 3.4:   DIY Tag Cloud 74
Figure 3.5:   Earthquake Map 76
Figure 3.6:   Image Doctoring 78
Figure 3.7:   Photo Before 79
Figure 3.8:   Photo After 79
Figure 3.9:   Palm 1 80
Figure 3.10:   Palm 2 80
Figure 3.11:   Palm 3 80
Figure 3.12:   Palm 4 80
Figure 3.13:   Midi Keyboard 82
Figure 3.14:   Midi Software 82
Figure 3.15:   Audacity 85
Figure 3.16:   Hitchhikr 90
Figure 3.17:   Wiki Aggregator 93
Figure 4.1:   IM Speak 104
Figure 4.2:   Authentic Assignment 105
Figure 4.3:   Format Rules 108
Figure 4.4:   Communication Rubric 107
Figure 4.5:   Blogging 110
Figure 4.6:   Wiki Diagram 111
Figure 4.7:   Graphics Features 114
Figure 4.8:   Editing an Image 115
Figure 4.9:   GIF Animation 118
Figure 4.10:   Bernoulli 118
Figure 4.11:   Water Cycle 119
Figure 4.12:   Content Management 125
Figure 4.13   HTML for Teachers 127
Figure 5.1:   Creative Commons Form 143
Figure 5.2:   Creative Commons Badge 144
Figure 5.3:   Authentic Assignments 146
Figure 5.4:   NSBA Report 154
Figure 6.1:   Shifts 160
Figure 6.2:   Speech from Second Life 162
Figure 6.3:   Personal Learning Network 166

Acknowledgments

This book owes its planning and execution to more people than I can possibly thank on one page. So I will list only a few. First, my thanks to my father, a true computer visionary. He recognized the potential of computers in the 1960s without an advanced degree in mathematics or engineering. Thanks also to my mother, who taught me to finish everything that I start, and to find joy in the doing.

As with all of my writing, I thank Paul Gilster, my neighbor and author of many books on science and technology. Continue to watch his work on interstellar space travel—Centauri Dreams. Google it!

A very special and loving thank you for my wife, Brenda, who had the courage to say, "Quit your job and let's see if we can make a living without it." In the same breath, I thank my daughter, Ryann, and son, Martin, two literate 21st century citizens.

A very special thank you to Cynthia Anderson, my project manager, and Marlene Woo-Lun, editor and president of Linworth Publishing. Their patience, humor, priceless advice, encouragement, and our many conversations about gadgets, have all served to keep me on task.

One final thanks to the crew at The Lassiter Starbucks, for their constant good humor and the dozens of espressos that they served with a smile.

About the Author

David Warlick's unique voice and message combine a wide range of experiences, both inside and outside the education arena. He ran two businesses before graduating from high school and spent more than a year in manufacturing before completing his undergraduate work. Mr. Warlick worked for nearly 10 years as a middle school social studies, math, and science teacher, during which time he also wrote award-winning instructional software and introduced hundreds of teachers to the educational potentials of personal computers.

Since 1995, Mr. Warlick has been the owner and principal consultant of The Landmark Project, a consulting and innovations firm in Raleigh, North Carolina. During this time David has spoken at conferences and delivered workshops for educators throughout the United States, Canada, and audiences in Europe, Asia, and South America.

Introduction

There has been no time in human history quite like this. Our world is changing more rapidly, and more of us are aware of it than ever before. The planet has never seemed so small, as we witness events around the world in real time through our televisions that are connected to a global network of cables and satellite communications, and increasingly through the computers on our desks, under our arms, and in our pockets. At the same time, our individual worlds, the people we know, and who know us, resources we have access to and use, conditions that influence our experiences, and those we affect with our actions have never been so great.

At no time was this sense of a shrinking globe and expanding personal experience more obvious than the day that we entered the 21st century and the world watched the first celebrations in the island nation of Kiribati, the first inhabited islands west of the International Date Line. Through the next 24 hours, we followed as each time zone marked the beginning of a new century with fireworks, celebration, and the sense of a dawning era.

The seemingly viral spread of conversation across the planet astounds us all, especially as people living in villages without running water, walk around with cell phones to their ears ("Cell Phone Boom in Rural Africa") and surf the Net with battery-powered notebook computers connected wirelessly to the World Wide Web (Markoff). Not only are we communicating with each other in ways that would have seemed pure science fiction only a few years ago, but the sheer vastness of the information that is available today through the World Wide Web overwhelms us all, as do the seemingly magical tools that assist us in searching for relevant information within a library of billions of documents and constantly growing and indexed conversations. Advances in genetic research, nanotechnology, and explorations of the universe and the inner workings of atoms are causing us to redefine our lives and experiences in fundamental ways.

Examples of breakthrough discoveries and technologies could more than fill this book. But it is, by the same token, important that we recognize that these advances are happening at a rate that renders them almost unnoticed. It was only a decade ago that we were largely limited to the information printed in books and stored in our libraries and classrooms, from which we taught our children about the world around them. Today, we take for granted the fact that we can casually use the World Wide Web to look up spur-of-the-moment interests, the answers to nagging questions, seek reliable references and casual comments, or research major topics that influence us all.

Our children seem especially immune to and oblivious of the unprecedented changes happening around us, while they seem to exemplify the new way of viewing the world through its information. This is especially evident when considering the gifts that children ask for at holidays. Instead of the array of model cars, balls and bats, dolls, and dress-ups we dreamed about while going through the Sears wish book, they long for information in the form of music on CDs and online music services, movies on DVDs, games on disk or cartridge, and the devices that play this information.

Since writing the first edition of this book, our students have taken even more control over their information experiences by subscribing to podcasts and their favorite YouTube artists, and sharing them with their friends and followers through a new genre of interactive Web sites called social networks.

For our children, information brings meaning to their personal and group experiences—even more so than technology. They understand a different value in information, not so much from its consumption (reading, viewing, listening), as from what they can do with the information, mixing and remixing content to create valuable and interesting new information products.

Our natural inclination is to be concerned about our children's preoccupation with information technologies, to worry that they are not learning to interact with real people in real circumstances. However, we are coming to understand that their information experiences are merely a new and extraordinarily broad conduit for interactions that far exceed those that we enjoyed in our younger relationships (Gunn). They do interact with each other face-to-face. But when they are not together, their conversations continue through instant messaging, text messaging, and their social networks (MySpace, Facebook, and Bebo).

Web Resources

http://youtube.com/
http://myspace.com/
http://facebook.com/
http://bebo.com/

Our job, as educators, is to prepare our students for their future. Today, this job is especially challenging, because for the first time in history, we cannot clearly describe that future. Our world is changing too fast. The very nature of information is changing, in . . .

- What it looks like,
- What we look at to view it,
- How and where we find it,
- What we can do with it, and
- How we communicate it.

At the same time that we grapple with the changing nature of information, we must also acknowledge that we are trying to accomplish our instructional goals in classrooms and libraries that sometimes owe more to the 19th century than a time with personal computers, the Internet, and a global library of content. They are production plants designed for industrial age processes, and we must learn to reshape them, to set new educational goals, for a new generation or species of learner, and a new and dynamic information landscape.

For the first time in years, important and powerful organizations are struggling with and identifying the new skills of a new future. The Partnership for 21st Century Skills ("Framework for 21st Century Learning"), the announcement of ISTE's National Educational Technology Skills for students ("ISTE NETS Refresh Project"), and the Workforce Readiness Report Card ("Are They Really Ready to Work?") are all focusing our attention toward:

- Creativity,
- Communication,
- Collaboration,
- Critical thinking,
- Decision making,
- Digital citizenship,
- Ethics,
- Diversity,
- Information fluency,
- Information technology application,
- Innovation,
- Lifelong learning
- Problem-solving,
- Research,

. . . and labeling these skills as "basic."

At the same time that we struggle to adapt education to a rapidly changing world, we, in the United States, continue to be held accountable to formally established sets of skills and content, as mandated by our governments in compliance with No Child Left Behind (NCLB) ("No Child Left Behind: A Desktop Reference"), standards that are based more steadfastly on the core literacies and content of the past two centuries. The phrase, *The 3Rs*, was coined in 1828 by Sir William Curtis, the Lord Mayor of London (Wikipedia Contributors, "The Three Rs"). For those adept at spelling, it should come as no surprise that the Honorable Lord Mayor was, himself, quite illiterate.

The purpose of this book is not to replace the three Rs, but to expand them to a model for literacy that applies to classrooms that are shape-shifting under the pressures of three converging conditions.

1. **For the first time in history, we are preparing our students for a future we cannot clearly describe.**

2. **Many of the students we are preparing enjoy and are accustomed to information experiences outside the classroom that are richer, deeper, and possibly more pedagogically appropriate to learning than their information experiences inside our schools.**

3. **The information landscape that we live and work within has changed dramatically.**

As we work to adapt our classrooms, teaching practices, and curriculums under the pressures of these converging conditions, we should recognize that each of these forces points to new ways of thinking about the education process, each suggesting strategies that may be helpful in retooling classrooms. Throughout this book, we will be exploring

- What this new information landscape means to our definition of literacy (adapting to a new information landscape),

- How our students' outside-the-classroom experiences might help us to turn literacy skills into information habits, harnessing our students' information experience and the energy it generates, and

- That perhaps the best thing we can be teaching our children today **is how to teach themselves** (how to learn what they need to know, to do what they need to do), that the literacy habits we want them to develop are actually *learning literacies*. (See Figure 0.1: Converging Conditions)

There is one call to education reform that will not be used in this book, a mantra that attendees to educational technology and media conferences often hear, that we should be *integrating technology* into our libraries and classrooms. It is an idea that is not without its usefulness. *Integrating technology* is a simple and inclusive way to describe the modernizing of our schools. However, *integrating technology* misses the point that technology has no special place in re-examining the pedagogy of teaching and learning. It is merely a tool—the pencil and paper of our time. It is ever changing and an almost impossible target to hold in the sites of curriculum development or our budgets.

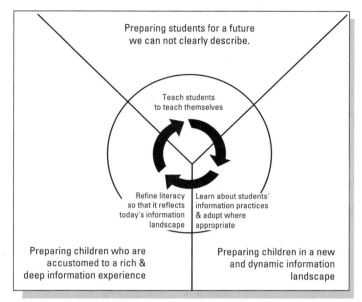

Preparing students for a future we can not clearly describe.

Teach students to teach themselves

Refine literacy so that it reflects today's information landscape

Learn about students' information practices & adopt where appropriate

Preparing children who are accustomed to a rich & deep information experience

Preparing children in a new and dynamic information landscape

Figure 0.1: Converging Conditions

On the other hand, information is a far more central element of our process, and the changing nature of information is more fundamental to what we do and our reform efforts. The skills and habits involved in using information to accomplish goals—literacy—are much more appropriate to our efforts as educators than practices in operating machines. **Educators should seek to integrate literacy, rather than integrate technology.** If we can rethink what it is to be literate in today's information environment, and integrate that, then the technology will come. But it will not come because we are convinced that laying our children's hands on these machines will make them smarter, or better prepared for their future. Computers and the Internet will be an essential part of teaching and learning because they are the tools of contemporary literacy.

User's Guide

There are several conventions that I will follow throughout this book in order to make it easier to use. First of all, and most importantly, I write from the perspective of a simple and fundamental definition of literacy.

I will organize and seek to describe the basic skills we need, and need to be teaching our children, that empower us to access, process, and communicate information in order to accomplish goals—within the context of today's information landscape.

> **" Literacy comprises those skills involved in using information to accomplish goals! "**

Throughout this book, I will emphasize or "double-click" large ideas that have given me pause and cause to rethink what I do and what I promote in my efforts to help retool schools and classrooms for the 21st century. I hope that they will give you ideas to think about and discuss with your colleagues, administrators, students, and their parents. You will know when we have encountered one of these large ideas when it is repeated as a sidebar in bolder text on the margin of the page.

In the early stages of planning this project, I decided not to emphasize the "how to" aspects of integrating a new literacy. Although there will be some points where I provide instructions and even diagrams, in most cases I will urge you to seek out someone with whom you work for guidance or collaboration as you work to teach yourself how to accomplish these tasks with the computers, software, and infrastructure you have in your school. Your guide or collaborator may be a fellow teacher, your library media specialist, or the school's technology facilitator. It may be your district network administrator, director of technology, or even a parent. Also, do not hesitate to ask your students. It probably would not surprise you that they know a lot about these new tools and harnessing the information, and we might profit from that fact as a point of conversation about tools, learning, and their future. This is actually the main reason that I suggest that you find a local expert to help you with technical tasks. It will give you and your colleagues a focal point for conversations about modernizing your classrooms and schools and how to accomplish that retooling on a continuing basis. It's one way to become, as an educator, a **master learner** and to model that element of being a citizen of the digital networked age.

Most chapters will end with **Action Items**, a list of suggested actions for library media specialists, teachers, administrators, parents, and students. If, after reading the chapter you ask yourself, "What do I do now?" this section will give you practical tips that you can enact today in your classroom, media center, school, or to begin to help it become a more artfully digital place.

This book also features an associated Wiki Web page, where readers can access presentation slides, links to blog entries about redefining literacy from the edublogosphere, online handouts for my conference presentations and workshops, various files associated with this book, and regularly updated Web links that began with the original edition of this book.

You can reach this Web site at:

http://davidwarlick.com/redefining_literacy

Finally, much of what is behind the book is a story about new schools, new classrooms, and new literacy. It is a simple story, in the same way that the 3Rs are a simple story. Jennifer James, a cultural anthropologist from Seattle and frequent keynote speaker at education technology conferences, often talks about leadership and the three kinds of effective leaders who affect change.

There is the leader who is so good at what she does that people are inspired to follow her lead and change their thinking in order to conform to this person's accomplishments. Think of Oprah Winfrey as an example of one who leads through sheer skill.

There is also the leader who is so creative and effective in giving us new ways of looking at our world and experience that people want to look in the same directions, alter their perceptions, and address problems with new solutions. Albert Einstein or Steve Jobs may be examples of leaders who exhibit this characteristic.

Finally, there is the leader who can tell a compelling new story. An excellent example was Ronald Reagan. He was not exceptionally skilled, and he was not particularly creative. But, he told a compelling story. For better or for worse, he changed much about this country and about the world because people were compelled to listen and believe (James).

There is a story about education that we all know. It is at the foundation of our culture, because it is the story of our own experiences of the 12 or 13 years that we all spent in classrooms listening to teachers, completing our worksheets, and cramming for tests. This story exercises enormous influence over how we teach and manage our classrooms today and the visions that our society aspires to in reforming education. We need a new story, one that represents a rapidly changing world, a new generation of learners—our children, and an information landscape that is both wondrously useful and surprisingly fragile.

The first chapter of this book is a story. This story has not happened—yet. It is a future fiction of a school in the future and what it might look like and how it might operate. I hope that you enjoy this and the other little stories that are included throughout this book as you learn about and implement this new literacy in your school with your students. This is our task as educators—to tell a new story about teaching and learning in the 21st century and to use this story to reshape our teaching and learning environment.

CHAPTER 1

A Day in the Life of School 2.0 – 2015

O ne of the most interesting and powerful aspects of this new information landscape, and the technologies that enable it, is its connectedness. When information is stored and organized in containers, its connections must happen intellectually through our own mental organizations.

Today, as information flows through a growing number of new applications, it tends to carry with it information about itself, enabling information to organize itself dynamically, as a function of its being and its flow.

This story tracks the flow and impact of a single piece of information through the day of a typical school in 2015.

The Story

Cesar Kelly reported to work on Monday with three major objectives on his mind. Hired as Clark Middle School's librarian, he was charged with reinventing the facility, which addresses ongoing national initiatives to integrate 21st century skills and work styles into its schools. Cesar had, in his view, the perfect job.

The first objective was to introduce a new RSS feed he had piped together over the weekend. Mary Copeland, a social studies teacher, had a team of students, the *Counters*, who were reproducing a 1990s news program about the Balkan Conflicts. The feed directed a variety of related news and blogs into a single RSS address. Cesar had already integrated the feed into *Feed Circus*, his own creation, a mashup site that integrated a wide variety of live topics into a single eclectic and weirdly entertaining digital news service. The *Feed Circus* had become increasingly popular with a broad and international audience, spawning a second news service that aggregates and displays only the reactions of *Feed Circus* readers.

More pressing, however, was getting the feed into the hands of the *Counters*, a shortening of the team's original name, *Counting on the fingers of Babbage*. Before reporting to the library, Cesar dropped by Mary Copeland's room, finding her at her desk computer, arranging content feeds to be displayed on the front wall of her classroom. She had already directed a local weather report, along with a report from the Hunan Province of China, home of one of their sister classes in the city of Zhengzhou. Also in Mary's room was a Webcam view of the sun rising over the Rockies and a radio station in Brazil playing through the classroom speakers.

Cesar walked across the room, sliding his tablet out of the canvas bag hanging from his shoulder. Laying it on the nano-textured surface of her desk, he asked if the *Counters* were still working on the Balkans project. Mary replied, "Yep!" Her attention was drawn immediately from the action on her class wall. Cesar knew that the *Counters* were a secret favorite of Mary's.

He directed her to the display on his tablet, saying, "Here's a feed that I piped together over the weekend." As she leaned forward to watch, he clicked open his profile, and unfolded his feed cloud, a structured listing of the content sources that he subscribed to and the more complex feeds that he constructed himself—a personal hobby. Clicking on the feed called News from the Balkans, a window unfolded, listing a variety of color-coded content objects, some of them formally published news items, and many of them blog postings.

"This is marvelous," Mary remarked, genuinely impressed. "Can we get into the construct, and tweak the feed?" Cesar rarely left the construct open, but for Mary, he did, knowing that she encouraged her students to customize their sources.

"I'll take it," she said, and Cesar dragged the feed over to an icon that opened his level one social network, where an icon representing the social studies teacher's profile—a caricatured face of Mary—appeared and automatically enlarged for him to drop the feed into. Because of the nature of his top level social network, all related feeds that he builds or captures in the future also will be shared into Mary's profile.

Gathering his tablet back up, Cesar sang, "Have a nice day," as he walked out of her classroom and turned toward the library. Mary opened the Balkans feed again into a corner of the 21-inch display on her desk and scanned through the items. After satisfying herself about its potential value to the *Counters'* project, she dragged it over to her student social network, and dropped it into the cloud for the *Counters*. It automatically found its way into the profiles of the appropriate team members and into the project profile.

Entering the library, Cesar dropped his bag on one of the work tables in the open space, which resembled a Kinko's. The young-looking 29-year-old had kept a few of the book cases, predominately those filled with fiction and classic reference materials, and replaced the rest with work spaces. They included round tables intended for group work, three interactive tables, work carrels, and other comfortable lounging furniture for reading and conversation.

He had converted the librarian's office into a conference room, so he customarily worked among the students. Cesar slid his thumb across a smooth black window on the 19-inch display, one inhabiting each of the work tables. Sliding his thumb across a black glassy square on the display, the young man caused the computer to recognize him, and to load his personal configuration, granting him access to the entire Internet.

Touching an egg-shaped icon on the screen, Cesar opened his profile, and then touched an icon of an illuminated manuscript to unfold a window that included the school's digital library. The entire school subscribed to a social bookmarking service that facilitated an enormous library of Web resources, contributed to by all of its members. The library was organized by tags, each resource tagged with words and phrases that describe them.

At its implementation, Cesar and his media committee had agreed on a set of tags that identified Clark Middle School, and the various teachers, grade levels, subject areas, and even various units taught by the teachers. As a result, RSS feeds could be constructed that channeled all current and continuing Web sites tagged with, for example, Clark Middle School, grade 8, social studies, and the unit on "Maps and Problem-Solving." The resulting dynamic list could be applied to the teachers' classroom Web site, blog, or the library's Wiki listing of relevant digital resources.

Working on a project about species support, Lien Chuang, a science teacher, had begun a listing of Web resources tagged to the school and also to efforts to protect nesting turtles on Folly Beach, South Carolina. Over the weekend, a note came in to Cesar, linked to that tag. It was from a member of a passion community that had formed around a Folly Turtles' Web site. Offering access to a wide range of resources and expertise, Cesar dragged the note over to Lien's profile, still attached to the feed for the Folly Beach efforts.

With only minutes left before students reported to class, Lien closed off a Skyped conversation with a relative in Shanghai, and opened her profile. Her eye was immediately drawn to the recent note forwarded to her from the library. She opened the note, read it, and then dragged it over to the profile of one of her student teams, the *Crustaceans*, with a request that they examine this passionate community, looking for ways they might contribute to the project.

As the bell rang, signaling the start of the first period of class, a group of sixth graders walked into the library and up to Mr. Kelly without saying a word. Cesar asked, "Are you the team *Sitting Bull* from Ms. McDonald's class?"

The smallest youngster, Cesar knew as Manabu, nodded and said, "She sent us down to start working on our game." Cesar and Kristin Mcdonell had been planning this project for a while, asking a team of students to design and develop a video game that would help players learn to choose nutritious foods.

"So, you've already laid out the game? You have a storyboard?"

Manabu sat his tablet on the table in front of the librarian, already queued to the storyboard. Cesar examined it briefly, having previously intercepted it from the team's social network, examining the layout, and commenting some suggestions.

"Very well. Follow me." Cesar led the four students over to an interactive table, a recent addition to the library that utilized surface computing and multi-touch technology. As they leaned over the black table, it glowed into action. Manabu, thumbed into the system, dragged out his social network, and tapped into the profile for their project. He then tapped out about two dozen images that appeared to spill out across the table. "These are our sprites," Manabu said.

Cesar thumbed into the computer, opened up a folder with applications, and dragged out one called *Alice*. "And here's your game development tool. Enjoy!" The youngsters all leaned in closer, dragging the digital pictures, the sprites, over to one corner of the table, making room for the software to unfold.

As Cesar thumbed back out of the computer, a buzz emerged from the group as they started to reason through the various motion, control, and sensing modules they could combine into their game. Cesar turned and walked away, leaving the team to teach themselves how to program the game. They'll come to him if they need help.

Meanwhile, Tulla Tijerina, one of the *Counters*, had discovered a blogger from Bosnia-Herzegovina, Lucija Ana Slatinek, who had written a series of short stories about life in Sarajevo during the conflicts. She shared some ideas with the other *Counters*, via their network, and Joey volunteered to check out her profile.

After finding no evidence that Lucija would be an inappropriate contact, the *Counters* arranged a meeting with Mrs. Copeland, to suggest that they write a screenplay for one of the author's short stories, and perform the story as a play, with Lucija's help, via Skype. Mary loved the idea, but cautioned the students that she must contact Ms. Slatinek first and talk through processes. The *Counters* were thrilled as they went back to their class work and continued their news production project.

Before the end of the day, Lien Chuang enjoyed an impromptu meeting with the *Crustaceans* to talk about their new idea—to hold a teleconferenced interview with the president of the Folly Beach Turtle Watch Program. She agreed that it was a fabulous idea, and that, after she had contacted the person, she would help them plan the interview.

Several weeks later, the *Crustaceans* delivered a report on the challenges of the Folly Beach turtles caused by the lights of the town. They included a recording of an interview with the president of the Folly Beach Turtle Watch Program, and other resources contributed by a large passion community of the plight of nesting sea turtles.

On the same day, a group of sixth graders delivered a presentation about their experiences in developing a video game about nutrition. They also discussed their lessons-learned, describing what they would do differently if they made another game, and they demonstrated the game for their audience. The game is now available in the school network and as a download.

At the end of the day, the *Counters* broadcasted a remake of a 1990s news story about the Balkans Conflicts with additional footage that they had inserted supporting part of the story and calling into question others. Along with that production they announced a future performance, with a screenplay written by the team based on a short story by Lucija Ana Slatinek, and co-directed by Lucija Ana Slatinek, of Bosnia-Herzegovina.

All of the performances were broadcast through the school's Web-based video station, and recorded as podcasts from the school's Web site and through Apple iTunes. It was enjoyed by parents and community members, one using a tablet in her home, several grandparents through their home computers, a number of community members with Internet feeds into their family TVs, and nine people using cell phones.

Learning, in 2015, will be about making connections.

Assumptions About the Future

This future fiction is only one speculative view among many possibilities that depend on a nearly endless number of variables. Writing the story was a unique and enlightening experience in itself. Guessing at the technologies that, though they are already available to some degree, may be widespread in the next five to 10 years, and then super-imposing a teaching and learning environment around those technologies caused me to reconsider a variety of issues related to education. It is essential, in this time of rapid change, that we add *futurist* to the job description of educator, and facilitate ongoing research, discussion, and reflection about the future for which we are preparing our children. (See Appendix C: Where to Find the Future)

At the same time that we consider the future, we should also be thinking about the technologies that will shape the learning environments that we will craft for our students. If you feel any sense of confidence in your mastery of the technologies of teaching and learning, then I suggest that you think about the following advancements.

> " The process of preparing our children for their future should involve holding their hands and personally guiding them into their future. "

Consider quantum computers, a brand new technology that is currently being researched and developed with some early success. The basis of quantum computing is its reliance on the behavior of quantum particles (electrons, protons, and particles even more fundamental and strange) to add, subtract, and remember things—the essence of computing. The benefit of quantum computing is that these machines would be able to operate at unimaginable speed. I use the word *unimaginable*, because at the quantum level, neither time nor distance exist. Therefore, many computations could be performed simultaneously, from a Newtonian perspective.

To stir things up even more, scientists in California, Canada, and Denmark are beginning to perform the first experiments in teleportation, causing an object in one location to suddenly appear in another (Shachtman). Scientists are even succeeding in creating matter by forcing sub-atomic particles to shape themselves into specific atoms and molecules, called designer matter (McCarthy). You may one day stand in front of a machine and say, "Earl Grey—Hot," and suddenly a quantity of vaporous gas turns itself into a piping hot drink served on an English tea service.

Now ask yourself, "How incredible does this sound, computers operating where time and space do not exist and the idea of Scottie beaming us around town?"

Hold that thought for just a moment.

Go back to 1993. The World Wide Web is in its infancy with only a handful of Web pages and none of them with pictures. Most of us have not even heard of the Internet. The author of a book, that you will one day read, steps into your classroom and suggests that your students soon will be walking into your classroom each morning with a laptop computer under their arms— multimedia computers that are more powerful than the largest mainframes of 1990—and that each of these computers will be connected to a global electronic library of billions of pages of text, pictures, graphs, sounds, animations, and even video, and that they may well be contributors to this global library on a daily basis. Then ask yourself if this suggestion in 1993 would have seemed any less incredible then, than my previous description of machines that work outside the limits of time and space.

We live in a time when only one or two decades can see literally unimaginable changes in the tools that we use to accomplish our goals and their impacts on society. At the same time, the basic fabric of our society changes much less quickly and with a greater deal of resistance—and this is fortunate. But teaching and learning through distance, using digital tools and resources, has become an essential part of our education landscape.

Distance learning solves important problems as we cope with the challenges of making a living in a rapidly changing and widening world. Michael Cox, the chief economist of the Federal Reserve Bank of Dallas, Texas, recently said to a group of students that they would ". . . have at least five jobs after (they) graduate, four of which have not been invented yet" (Mokhoff). According to the U.S. Bureau of Labor Statistics, citizens born from 1957 to 1964 held, on average, 10.2 different jobs from age 18 to 38 ("Younger Boomers"). If any variation of this trend is correct, then being able to learn from any place and at any time will be part of prospering in the future.

However, it is important that our children prepare for their future within personal face-to-face relationships. Socialization is an act of sharing, guiding, and nurturing. But the relationship must be richer than a teacher who simply delivers instruction, with students passively receiving and storing that instruction.

> **" For the first time in history, our job, as educators, is to prepare our students for a future that we cannot clearly describe. "**

Assumptions—New Tools

It is actually quite astonishing how many of the technologies, described in the more forward-reaching 2003 version of this story, have come to pass in some way by 2008. New Web based applications and computing devices have emerged that we simply were not thinking about only a few years ago. Today, laptop classrooms, where each student has access to a fast multimedia computer connected wirelessly to the global Internet, are becoming commonplace. We are also starting to see a new breed of computer, the UMPC (Ultra Mobile Personal Computer), which approaches the capabilities of the tablets mentioned in the story.

These highly portable machines provide the access to information and information tools that self-learners need. We must all have ubiquitous and convenient access to digital and networked information at the point that a student (or teacher) needs it. Saying that a learner can share a networked computer with 30 other students in her class is as ridiculous today as saying that they must share a single textbook with dozens of readers.

Another assumption related to the technology we will be using is that information becomes more valuable when it is delivered most efficiently. As highly as we regard reading, most of us spend an enormous amount of time watching video in the form of TV programming, commercials, or movies. We also view images, animations, and listen to information being spoken to us. Well-produced video is compelling, as are carefully rendered images, graphs, and animations. We should be able to utilize these media formats much more freely and frequently, and the required technology should be an integral part of every classroom. The tools to communicate effectively with students should not have to be *checked-out* from the media center.

Today, more and more classes are equipped with ceiling mounted digital projectors and many have permanently mounted interactive white boards that enable the operation of the classroom computer from the board at the front of the room, by touch. In fact, there are a number of companies that are currently marketing e-paper, nearly paper-thin material that serves as a computer display, able to reprint itself based on instructions from a computer. E-paper can be rolled up or pasted to any flat surface. Consider electronic wallpaper in your classroom where you could display content on any wall or other flat surface, cheaply.

The holy grail of digital publishing appears to be the point where e-paper can be produced more cheaply than pulp-based paper. There are a wide range of predictions of when this may happen, but consider that at this writing, you can purchase a Sony E-Paper eBook for $299 USD, with a free download of 100 books. Calculating the cost of 100 print books at $6 a copy for paperbacks, the information is being delivered digitally at half the cost of cutting down trees.

> " What will our libraries become, when all knowledge is available through personal information devices – anytime, anyplace, a mouse click away? "

Finally, in this school (and our communities) of 2015, the information will be in the air. Wireless access to content will be almost ubiquitous. It has already begun. Large parts of this book were written in coffee houses, airports, and hotel lobbies where the Internet is freely accessed with a wireless-equipped notebook computer. The range of access available to the notebook computer being used to write this book recently increased dramatically with the addition of an AT&T USBConnect air card, which plugs into a USB port and enables access to the Internet through the growing forest of cell towers that pepper our terrain.

This increasing access to a world of knowledge begs the question, "What will our libraries become, when all knowledge is available through personal information devices—anytime, anyplace—just a mouse click away?" Hold that thought.

Assumptions—How the Information Flows

Perhaps the greatest advances seen since the writing of the first edition of this book are how digital networked content flows. We are now cultivating personal libraries through our RSS aggregators that, instead of our going out and finding information, we are literally training the information to find us.

We are also beginning to visit each other's classrooms and invite guest speakers to present through the networks using video of quite acceptable quality, and broadcasting our classes through Web-based video broadcasting services. Recently, an independent school on the east coast of the United States broadcast their students' presentations to parents and interested educators using a free service called USTREAM.

Recently, I received notification, via a Twitter message, that Dean Shareski, a Canadian educator, was delivering a conference presentation on self-publishing and broadcasting the session using USTREAM. In the next few minutes, educators from Scotland to Shanghai were watching this presentation and discussing the topic using the USTREAM chat feature.

After a moment, Dean described to his attendees that he was broadcasting the conference session, and asked if any of the virtual attendees had anything to share about the subject. I volunteered and Skyped into the presentation so that I could describe various self-publishing services available now (see Figure 1.1: Virtual Presentation). Expanding conference presentations across the continents and accepting input from a global audience has become an almost every day experience.

Web Resources

http://ustream.tv/
http://skype.com/
http://voicethread.com/

Figure 1.1: Virtual Presentation

Increasingly, students are collaborating in their classrooms using Wikis, publishing to local and distant audiences with blogs, and commenting on multimedia productions using new tools such as Voicethread—and this is only what they are doing in their classrooms. We are only now starting to understand the social networking that they are doing outside their classrooms.

The story told earlier in this chapter tries to make more sense of social networking within the context of education. Social networks, as they are used today, typically consist of a profile, surrounded by a variety of communication tools that connect the user to friends and colleagues. The profile describes the user and shares favorite books, movies, music, photos, and other relics of the user's activities.

The problem with this arrangement is that the social networking service, such as MySpace or Facebook, serves as a container, preventing interactions across networks. For instance, it is difficult to impossible for a user in Facebook to interact with a user of MySpace or one of the popular education networks on Ning. The use of social networks in this story is slightly different, where our profiles are separate from any particular network. As a separate entity, the profile can share permissible aspects of the user with other profiles and networks, and even grow dynamically, based on the information behaviors of the user.

As a result, networks can be formed and cultivated, such as a network of the other teachers in your school, a network of other librarians in your district, or high school librarians around the world. Temporary networks can be formed around specific projects and more permanent ones around passion communities.

Web Resources

http://facebook.com/
http://myspace.com/
http://ning.com/

Dynamic profile-to-profile interactions through our networks become a critical part of how we accomplish our goals, both professionally and personally. Containers go away and are replaced by rich and growing networks of users.

Assumptions—What We Do with New Tools

Some assumptions will be more difficult to achieve than inventing and even procuring new technologies. They apply less to what appears in the classroom and more to our practices of teaching and learning. They depend less on the market-driven advance of technology, and more on people's willingness to invest in fundamental changes in schools and schooling.

As we move toward personal information devices, our *tablets*, and away from 20 and 30-pound book bags, there will be an increasing market for dynamic digital learning products that our students will use anywhere, any time. At the same time, as teachers and students become more accustomed to the volumes of information that are available on the Internet, the extreme flexibility of digital information, and as we become more literate in terms of networked, digital, and abundant information, we could see a major shift regarding what we now call textbooks. Traditionally, textbooks have been prebundled products, selected by state departments of education, and simply consumed by students. In the future, teachers and librarians will have a much more active role in what their textbooks contain and even how they behave.

Curriki, a play on the combination of *curriculum* and *Wiki*, is one current project that provides a space for educators to contribute their own teaching and learning resources. We can upload resources, such as texts, images, video or audio files, and even write and contribute textbooks and entire curricula. We can also take the resources contributed by others, and combine them into customized learning products for our students. Curriki operates under a concept called Open Source Curriculum (OSC), which invites a community of practitioners to contribute freely editable content—the community collaborating to build curriculum.

A similar upcoming service, Flat World Knowledge, provides textbooks in either print, digital, audio, and by chapter. In addition, teachers can rearrange chapters and even edit the texts, making their own professional edition of the book available for students as networked digital content, or to be ordered in print.

As educators start to collaborate in developing learning materials for their classes, students may also join in the effort customizing their own digital learning resources based on their personal interests and learning styles.

Web Resources

http://curriki.org/
http://flatworldknowledge.com/

Assumptions—Curriculum and the New Tools

Imagine a typical information age workplace. As you look around, you are probably standing inside a cubical with Dilbert cartoons taped on the wall. We will not disturb the cartoons, but as you look down, you see a telephone lying on the desk and plugged into the wall. As you consider this phone, chances are great that you have a cell phone in your pocket, attached to your belt, or lying in your purse. In fact, you may have already dropped your landline at home because you found it to be redundant to the cell phones that every member of your family carries with them. A recent National Center for Health Statistics report found that 12.8 percent of U.S. households rely solely on cell phones for communication, up from only 3.2 percent in 2003, when the first edition of this book was written. For people in the 25 to 29 age bracket, 29.1 percent no longer use landlines (Kim). The phone on our workspace desk disappears.

We continue to look around and see a number of bins, each labeled and holding stacks of paper. There are also a number of bound reports stacked on a shelf hanging from one of the walls. As we examine these papers and reports, consider a study conducted by The School of Information Management and Systems of the University of California at Berkeley. One of their findings was that in 2002 we generated five exabytes of new information. That much information would fill 37,000 Libraries of Congress. The kicker, however, is that only 0.01 percent (that is one one-hundredths of one percent) of that information is ever printed ("Executive Summary"). The remainder of the information is machine-readable. If the information that we are generating today is almost exclusively digital, then we will remove the papers and bound reports from our cubicle.

Excerpt from original version of this book:

> Several years ago, I was invited to tour The Media Lab at MIT. Stewart Brand, in his book, *The Media Lab*, called it the place where they are, ". . . inventing the future." As I was led around this building, designed by the architect, I.M. Pei, I was struck by its presence. The sole purpose of this building was to invent, using tools and concepts about which most people have never heard. One of the items that almost immediately caught my attention were the tiny video cameras that I saw, mounted on pencil-thin support rods, stationed at nearly every work area. They stood on every desk, coffee table, and work surface; every place where people might work included one of these quarter-sized cameras. I also noticed that nearly every lab and office held a large multimedia display. Often there were projectors mounted on the ceiling, but in many cases there were plasma style flat panels hanging on the wall.

The paragraph above, from the first edition of this book, was intended to impress readers with how people in the esoterically high-tech places of the world were starting to engage in casual multimedia communications regardless of distance. As this text is being written, a tiny video camera is embedded in this MacBook computer, and from this coffee shop I could call up and video teleconference educator friends in Illinois, New Brunswick, Wisconsin, California, and Georgia, which does not include my colleagues in Shanghai, Hong Kong, and Bangkok that I would be required to wake up. K-12 librarians and teachers are doing this every day today. There will be no need for extra chairs in our workplace of the future, so we can remove them.

Scanning around further we find a desktop computer sitting in a corner with a slide-out keyboard and mouse stand. Yet, today, we could easily replace that machine with a sleek laptop that has nearly the screen size and computing power, and the added benefit of being transportable. Futurists predict that we will soon be wearing our technology. This has already begun as many of us carry small computers and communication devices in our pockets, on our belts, or attached to our ears.

However, we may soon be wearing technology as jewelry, embedded in our eyeglasses, or stitched into our clothing. These devices will constantly be in contact with each other, sharing pertinent information, and talking not only with the devices on our person, but also with other appliances, such as our refrigerator or the engine in our cars.

That desktop computer disappears. No need. We carry our information technology with us.

So, what do we have left in our information age work area?

Almost nothing.

And this is exactly what we know about the future for which we are preparing our students—Almost Nothing.

For the first time in history, our job, as educators, is to prepare our students for a future that we cannot clearly describe. This idea has profound implications in terms of what our children should be learning, and even more importantly, how they should be learning it.

Critical Question for Educators and Communities

Considering our task in preparing our children for their future, a fundamental question that faces us as educators and as communities is, "What do children need to be learning today to be prepared for an unpredictable future?"

Perhaps the best thing we can teach them is how to teach themselves, and anyone who is literate has the skills to learn what they need to know, to do what they need to do. The purpose of this book is to expand our notions of what it means to be literate in the 21st century, where information is increasingly networked, digital, and overwhelming. This book does not define an additional information literacy, digital literacy, or techno-media literacy, but a redefinition of the basic skills, what we might call *Contemporary Literacy* (Friensen). It reaffirms the essence and vital importance of reading, writing, and basic mathematics, but refines them within the context of an information environment that is: digital, global, indexed, hyper-organized, multimedia, ubiquitous; and a future political, economic, and personal experience that is largely driven by that information. We will describe basic skills, not as the 3Rs but with three Es. (See Figure 1.2: 3E Literacy)

Gail Morse, one of the original Christa McAuliffe educators (Geiger), says that we were "paper-trained" in our classrooms, taught to use paper. Today, our students must be "light-trained."

Bring on the light!

	20th Century Literacy	**Contemporary Literacy**
Expose What Is True	Reading what someone handed to us	Exposing meaning and value from the information we encounter from a new and dynamic information landscape
Employ the Information	Basic mathematical skills.	Mathematics and refined skills of working the full range of content through the ones and zeros embedded in almost all information today
Express Ideas Compellingly	Writing	Expressing ideas fluently and compellingly with text, images, sound, video and animation

Figure 1.2: 3E Literacy

CHAPTER 2

Exposing What
Is True

For Christmas of 2000, George Warlick gave each of his family members, including me, a copy of the book he had worked on over the past year. The book was entitled, *What I Know about My Ancestors*. It was not a long book. There is not that much to tell. However, it was fascinating to read through the stories from his research and family legends going back to Johann Daniel Warlick's arrival in America in the early 18th century.

Following the generations through the decades, one impression persisted. Having settled in a rural part of the western piedmont of North Carolina, situated many miles from the nearest town, it is unlikely that they had access to books, pamphlets, or newspapers. There were very little media in their lives. Yet, education was very important to the family. Sons were customarily sent to a boarding school in Pennsylvania for high school. My grandfather and one of his brothers earned college degrees, the classics at the University of North Carolina and engineering at North Carolina State University. But despite this unusual regard for education, they still had little information available to them on a daily basis.

So what did education mean then and there? What did it mean to be educated in a time and place where published content was scarce? Education was a process of assuring that knowledge was learned and remembered. Being educated meant that you held a great deal of information in your memory, and that you gained that knowledge largely through reading, listening, and reciting within a formal and regimented educational setting.

Today, we find ourselves in an environment that is radically different, a world that is dominated by information. The very physical environment that we live in is largely defined by information, and we interact with that environment using information. An increasing amount of that environment-defining information is online, and this trend will certainly continue.

Consider a journey we might take from Raleigh to Boston to attend a conference. If we were driving, at the time of the first edition of this book, we would most likely have gone to a Web site to plot our course, receiving practical and printable turn-by-turn instructions taking us from central North Carolina to the door of the convention center. If we had decided to spend the night in Pennsylvania, and we collect Priority Points from Holiday Inn, we would visit their Web site for a list of hotels on the route, with photos, amenities, and prices. We might then reserve the room online and receive a map with the hotel's location. If we have a preference for the southern cooking of Cracker Barrel, we could visit their site to pinpoint their locations and plan our meal times. There may even be state department of transportation Web sites that identify problem areas of road construction and high congestion times offering real time video from Webcams along the way. To top it off we could shop for a good mystery book, purchase it, and download the book from the Internet as an MP3 file, so that we could be entertained during our travel.

Today, things have become even more interesting, where we simply get in the car, attach our portable GPS device to the front windshield, just to the right of the rear view mirror. After packing my luggage and a six-pack of spring water, we would dial in the address of the conference hotel in Boston, stored in our mobile phone calendar, which it automatically downloaded from our Google Calendar.

We hop in the car, and GPS starts telling me where to turn and how far we'll travel before the next turn. As we become hungry, we pull off the road, press a few buttons on the GPS, asking it to find, in the vicinity of a town about 20 minutes down the road, our favorite pizzeria. It finds one, we call the number, pre-order a small pie with double mushrooms and peppers, and then press [go] on the GPS. It directs us to the pizza shop where our pizza is piping hot and ready.

A few hours later, we've decided to stop for the night in the Lancaster, Pennsylvania, area. Again, we pull off the road, press some buttons, and request the GPS to find the closest Courtyard by Marriott. We call, make a reservation, give them my Honors number, and we're on our way. Running low on gas? We can get a list of the closest service stations, which constantly shifts and refreshes as we continue up I-95. As we approach Philadelphia, our mobile phone runs a Google map tool that can show us highways that are currently congested. We decide to take a different route around the city, or simply detour into rural Pennsylvania, and the GPS continues to reroute me to the final destination. The world, in a sense, has become hyperlinked and it is linked by information.

Much of this world connecting information will not be exclusively intended for human consumption. Perhaps the next refrigerator that you purchase will be able to detect the expiration date of your milk, politely reminding you to replace it. Merloni Elettrodomestici, a maker of home appliances in Italy, currently produces a refrigerator that will display messages on a front panel, such as, "Eat the yogurt on the bottom shelf within one day." The next generation will order more yogurt from the store and have it delivered to your home based on your schedule, which it will access from the mobile phone in your pocket. All of this will be told to you the next time you enter your kitchen, or your fridge might just call you on your mobile phone and leave a message.

The point is that information will be vast, diverse, immediately available to knowledgeable and skilled information consumers, and it will be digital. There is a significant difference not only between the quantity of content available to us compared to my ancestors, but also in the characteristic of the information. For my ancestors, information was expensively stamped or scratched onto paper. Today, it is coded into ones and zeros, mass duplicated and transmitted, practically independent of time and space, almost without cost. Much of this change has occurred since we attended school, some of us in the 1950s and '60s, long before personal computers, CD-ROMs, the Internet, and mobile telephones.

We were taught literacy so that we could read the text that someone handed to us. We were taught to read the textbook provided by the teacher, the reference books to which the school librarian guided us. We were taught to read the newspapers and magazines that were sold to us by publishers. We were taught to read what somebody, whom we trusted, handed to us. In that information environment, merely being able to read and understand the text was sufficient to be called literate.

In the 21st century, literacy involves not just reading and comprehending the text in front of you. It now includes a range of skills to find, navigate, access, decode, evaluate, and organize the information from a globally networked information landscape. Almost all of the information that our students use in their future will be viewed with some type of information device (a computer), and it will

> " In the 21st century, Literacy…now includes a range of skills to find, navigate, access, decode, evaluate, and organize the information from a globally networked information landscape. "

come from a global electronic library that will be vast, largely unorganized and unmanaged, and produced from a bewildering variety of perspectives. If all our children learn to do is read, they will not be literate.

A Brief History of Networked Digital Information

The earliest beginnings of the Internet happened before some of us graduated from college and started teaching. Although we started using modems and e-mail in the middle 1980s, many of us did not hear about the Internet until the 1990s. There was a time when all of the K-12 educators on the Internet knew each other personally.

In 1990, if you wanted to access information from this "network of networks," you had to use a program called FTP, an abbreviation for File Transfer Protocol. It looked like DOS, a series of cryptic commands that you typed into the computer to list, move, or copy files from one computer's hard drive to another. The exhilaration came from the fact that these computers could be thousands of miles apart. We were wizards with the secret incantations to transport information around the world.

It is important to realize that this all happened before most of our students were born. It happened after some of us started teaching. But even more dramatic changes have occurred within the recollection of our high school students and since the first edition of this book was published. A suite of new Web applications has surfaced, so changing how we think about information that we've started to call it Web 2.0.

Many suggest that this new Web first appeared with the introduction of Google, the most popular search engine on the Internet, according to Search Engine Watch (Burns). If you remember your first experiences with Google, you were probably initially impressed with its clean minimal appearance. But just after that, you discovered that the quality of the Web sites surfacing to the top of the list of hits was much greater than you were accustomed to with Alta Vista and Yahoo. Google accomplished this by ranking its finds, not based on information provided by the publisher of the site, but by the number of other Web sites that linked to it. The recommendations from the Web publishing community began to determine value. This idea of content and value based on the behavior of a community is central to Web 2.0, and also represents another reason for us to re-evaluate contemporary literacy.

Web Resources

http://google.com/
http://altavista.com/
http://yahoo.com/

Another seminal date was August 23, 1999, when Pyra Labs introduced Blogger, a blog publishing tool that was free and available to anyone with access to the Web. Suddenly, people could publish their experiences, ideas, beliefs, fears, loves, and opinions to a world of potential readers. Prior to Pyra Labs' pivotal introduction, publishing was enormously expensive. The Web brought the cost down. But to share content with a Web-using audience required a Web server with hard disk space and the skills to code your content so that it could be viewed with most Web browsers—or the ability to hire someone with the skills to code your content. With Blogger, anyone who could access the Web from a public library, could set up a blog in less than 10 minutes, and be publishing blog articles before getting up. Pyra hosted the articles on their servers for free.

The word *blog* is a shorting of *Web log* and the *blogosphere* or *blogsphere* is a growing layer of the Web inhabited by blogs. It is where any person can have his say. Dave Sifry, the CEO of Technorati, a search engine of the blogosphere, publishes a quarterly report on the state of blog space in his blog, Sifry Alerts. In April of 2007, Sifry reported that . . .

> Technorati is now tracking over 70 million Weblogs, and we're seeing about 120,000 new Weblogs being created worldwide each day. That's about 1.4 blogs created every second of every day (Sifry, "The State").

Each quarter, the report includes a number of graphs that indicate the growth of the medium and information about the topics people are blogging about. In one graph, Sifry lists the top 50 read media sources for the first quarter of 2007, nine of which were blogs, which are published regularly at no cost. For instance, the popular technology and media blogs Engadget and Boing Boing enjoy more readers than *Businessweek*. Gizmodo and TechCrunch outranked the *Chicago Tribune*.

The authors of these blogs are obviously smart people who provide a valuable service, or else they would not be serving this many readers. But in what ways are our notions of literacy affected when content can be created, shared, read, watched, and listened to by a global audience with none of the traditional filters that we have relied on?

Although blogging, as we know it today, started with Pyra Labs in 1999, it did not enter the radar of educators until 2004, when educator, blogvangelist, author, and public speaker, Will Richardson introduced us to the instructional applications and implications of blogging at the National Educational Computing Conference in New Orleans, after the first edition of this book

Web Resources

http://blogger.com/
http://sifry.com/alerts/
http://engadget.com/
http://boingboing.net/
http://gizmodo.com/
http://techcrunch.com/

was published. The information landscape has become much more interesting with the entrance of Web 2.0.

Another cornerstone of the new information environment is the Wiki, and the most famous Wiki is Wikipedia. Launched on January 15, 2001, by Internet entrepreneur Jimmy (Jimbo) Whales and encyclopedian Larry Sanger, Wikipedia utilizes a free and open source Wiki server to maintain a free and growing encyclopedia, which anyone can edit. The definition, according to Wikipedia, is . . .

A Wiki is a collaborative Web site which can be directly edited by anyone with access to it (Wikipedia Contributors, "Wiki").

Its growth has been nothing less than a phenomenon, offering 2.46 million articles in English at this writing, with another 4.5 million articles from the nine next most frequently used languages, with 250 other languages using the site to describe their worlds. According to Alexa, a Web information company, Wikipedia is, at the time of this writing, number eight in the top 10 visited Web sites on the Internet ("Top Sites").

> **What kind of questions are we going to ask our students when they are entering our classrooms with Google in their pockets?**

The nature of information is dramatically different from how it looked and behaved when most of us were students. Consider that, according to U.S. Department of Education's Digest 2003-2004 data ("Highest Degree Earned"), more than a quarter of today's teachers were in education school more than 20 years ago. The percentage of U.S. teachers with 10 to 20 years of experience in the classroom is another 28.4 percent. These highly educated (48 percent with graduate degrees) and dedicated teachers are working in an information landscape that not only didn't exist, but wasn't even imagined when we graduated from college—32 years ago for me.

If young teachers, coming directly from our schools of education, had received more training in strategies for teaching and assessment techniques that reflect a networked, digital, and overwhelming information environment, then there would be more promise for classrooms adapting to dramatically changing conditions. Sadly, with a few exceptions, they are not. Young teachers may be more aware of the new landscape, as many of them sport Facebook profiles, text message as a matter of common conversation, and spend a significant amount of their recent years mastering complex video games. But seeing the intersections between an emerging and shifting information landscape and the info-architecture of curriculum, seems as unlikely for first and second year teachers as for 10 and 20 year educators.

Web Resources

http://wikipedia.org/
http://alexa.com/
http://facebook.com/

Decades ago, we struggled with calculators, an increasingly ubiquitous device that virtually cancels out the need for long division and calculating square roots. Eventually, calculators were admitted into math classes, and are now essential for many high school mathematics courses. They are also allowed during parts of SAT exams. Some time in the next five years our children are going to have every reason to expect to be able to bring the same information technologies into their classrooms that they are accustomed to using outside their classrooms. We have less than that amount of time to discover and to invent ways for channeling effective learning through the information tentacles that are their cell phones, networked video games, handheld computers, and other information technologies that are part of their daily digital conversations. We have less than that amount of time to decide what kinds of questions we are going to ask on their tests, when our students are walking into their classrooms with Google in their pockets.

In the published print information environment, to access information you had to be able to read. There were additional skills that we were taught, such as the ability to use a table of contents and an index. We were taught how to rely on the alphabet to locate information in an encyclopedia and other reference works and how to decode the Dewey Decimal System to navigate libraries. But most of the information that we accessed started with a single report, book, instruction guide, newspaper, or magazine. The chief and single defining element of literacy was *reading*, the ability to effectively and efficiently decode written or printed text.

Today, however, we rarely begin with a single book, newspaper, or magazine, or even set of reference books. When we are using information to accomplish our goals we now start with Google. Neither Google nor Yahoo publish the total number of Web documents that they index. However, according to the Web Server Survey, published by NetCraft, there were, as of March 2008, 162,662,052 distinct Web sites on the Internet—an increase of 40 million sites since June 2007 ("March 2008 Web Server Survey").

The fact that we might be able to access this much information from our pockets has profound implications on the skills needed to use information to accomplish goals. It dramatically expands what it means to be literate. Unless my children know how to locate information that is appropriate to what they are trying to achieve, I might prefer that they not know how to read.

> " Unless my children know how to locate information that is appropriate to what they are trying to achieve, I might prefer that they not know how to read. "

Finding the Information—Hypertext Environments

Before we begin exploring strategies for finding information on the Internet, it is important to take another look at the nature of Net-based information. We were taught to read in two dimensions—across and down. Today, we are increasingly reading in a third dimension: across, down, and deeper into the information (See Figure 2.1: 3-Dimensional Reading). By clicking through words, phrases, and images, we are able to dig into the information, moving deeper into greater understanding, or into greater distraction.

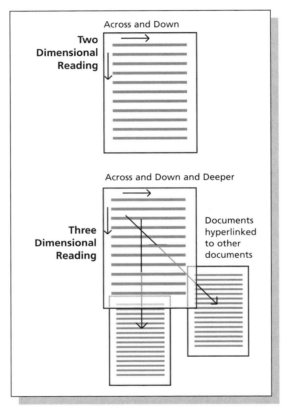

Figure 2.1: 3-Dimensional Reading

This 3-D arrangement adds value to the message you are trying to deliver in that it points to supporting documents, and related documents can point to yours. Its depth and richness can also lead to unrelated content that deflects us from our goals.

Many of our students are quite familiar and even adept at navigating hypermedia environments. Many of them have been navigating Web sites and hypermedia video games since they were only a few years old, and recently, they have been creating rich, complex social networks, using these environments as a means of communicating and collaborating with each other. But even though they seem experienced with navigating hypermedia environments, developing practices in the interest of learning should become a part of classrooms, even in the earliest grades. It is also important to acknowledge that not all students are becoming so skilled at using networked information environments. Let's hope that this inequity ceases to be a problem by the time a third edition of this book is necessary.

It may be inappropriate to direct kindergarteners and first graders into complex information environments. However, starting to learn about the effective use of 3-D information arrangements can easily be modeled by teachers.

We use media to help our young children learn about their world and their place in the world. This includes images, sound, video, animation, and text. Increasingly, these media are being displayed from computers, connected to the Internet, through digital projectors, and mounted permanently to the ceilings of our classrooms.

Instead of starting with the picture or video, the teacher might begin with the search engine or the front page of the Web site, from which the picture was found. Then the teacher can demonstrate the process of clicking through to the picture, perhaps even demonstrating false turns, and talking through the reasoning for clicking into relevant pages and away from less relevant pages. Young students need to learn that part of using information today involves the navigation of that information. It involves making decisions.

For older students, we might help them to better understand a 3-D information landscape by asking them to express what they are learning through hypertext and hypermedia environments that they construct. There are a number of social networking sites that are designed for instructional applications and with safety in mind. The following companies exhibited at the 2007 National Educational Computing Conference in Atlanta, Georgia, and included social networking in the description of their products.

- First Class

- Imbee

- TakingITGlobal

- Elgg

These are Web sites that enable or empower students to build and maintain personal information environments that represent themselves and their learning. They can be used for submitting work. They can also be used to facilitate collaboration between students.

Web Resources

http://firstclass.com/
http://imbee.com/
http://tiged.org/
http://elgg.org/

Wikis also can easily be used by students to create their own hypermedia documents. Civics is traditionally learned by listening to the teacher and reading the textbook assignments. In Chad Ball's middle school social studies class in Fredericton, New Brunswick, Canada, students are learning by building hypertext information environments. Mr. Ball first creates a Wiki site, which his students use as a reference for accessing information about government. Then he assigns teams of students to invent their own political parties and construct their own Wiki Web sites that include the party motto, logo, position papers, platforms, speeches, and candidate profiles for their party. Students from other classes then vote for the party they like the best, based on their explorations of the Wiki sites.

Ian Foggarty, a high school physics and biology teacher in the same city, stopped handing out lab manuals, when he was introduced to Wikis. Today, his students are required to write their own lab manuals that become available to other students. His students take pride in the value of their work. One team hired a tech-savvy friend to add interactive flash elements to their manual, paying for his services with cartons of chocolate milk.

Some schools are still prevented, by policy, from participating in social networks. Still, students can construct hypertext environments using many of the popular word processing programs they are already using in class, including Microsoft Word, iWorks, and OpenOffice.

As an example, your third grade class might be asked to read a story about Samantha's visit to the zoo. You have typed the story into a word processor so that as the students read at their computers; they have access to the word processor's features. You might ask the students to browse through one of the kid-friendly Web directories or search engines and select a Web page that corresponds with each of the animals they read about. Then they can turn the story into a hypertext document by converting the names of the animals in the story into hyperlinks that connect to the animals' Web pages. Add depth to the assignment by asking students to learn one thing about each animal from the Web page that they link to, and add what they learn to the text of the story. (See Figure 2.2: Hyperlinks)

Students could then save their hypertext stories on disk, share them with classmates, or take them home for their parents. The students' files also can be saved as Web pages and posted for community use, showing how your students are adding to the World Wide Web.

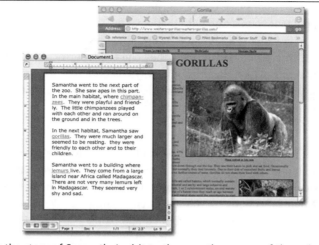

In the story of Samantha's visit to the zoo, the names of the animals are hyperlinked to web pages about the animal. To accomplish this:
1. Highlight the word you wish to make a hyperlink
2. Right mouse click on the word and select Hyperlink
3. On the window that appears, paste or type the URL of the page you want to link to
4. Click Screen Tip to enter a note that will pop out when the student places the pointer over the hyperlink
5. Click OK

Figure 2.2: Hyperlinks

Investigative Strategies—Personal Digital Libraries

The first strategy for searching the Internet for information is not really a search strategy. It is a library strategy. You probably have a personal library of professional books from college courses or graduate school, or books that you have purchased at workshops and conferences. You keep these books together and organized in one place because they consistently have information that helps you do your job.

Keeping a personal digital library is just as important and for exactly the same reason. You probably keep bookmarks or favorites on your computer, and you may organize them into folders and subfolders based on what you typically do when using the Web. You may organize them by the subjects you teach or your class periods. You may also have sub-folders for various units that you teach. You keep these bookmarks because they link to Web sites that consistently have information that helps you do your job.

The Internet is a big place that is constantly changing both in its content and how we go about connecting with that content. Teachers especially do not have time to conduct deep research every time they seek out content for their next unit of instruction. However, if they can easily keep and cultivate a personal digital library and organize it in ways that are personally and professionally meaningful, these online libraries become a very effective and vital first place to look for information.

The key to keeping bookmarks that are truly useful is organization. It is easy to do, adds value to your information, and you tend to take advantage of the information more frequently. Instructions for organizing browser bookmarks vary between Windows, Mac OS, and Linux computers, and across the versions of Microsoft Internet Explorer, Firefox, and other Web browsers. If you cannot figure it out, offer your tech facilitator some cookies so that she will show you how. For the most part, it is a matter of dragging the Web URL of a useful page from the address box into the appropriate bookmark folder or dragging a hyperlink into the appropriate folder.

In Figure 2.3, folders have been created for the teacher's two subjects: World Civilizations and U.S. History. The U.S. History folder is open, revealing subfolders for three units: Exploration, Colonial, and Revolution. The Colonial folder is open so that as she researches the Internet for appropriate Web sites, all she has to do is grab the link to "The 13 Colonies of America" Web site and drag it into the folder. It is a simple task, as simple as placing a book on a bookshelf, and the resource is available to the teacher from this point on within the context of what and how she teaches.

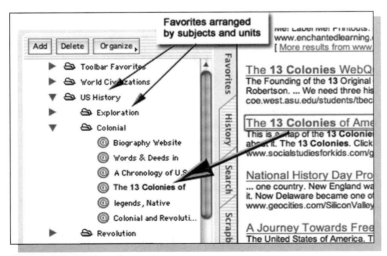

Figure 2.3: Bookmarks

Browser-based bookmarks, however, present a problem for many educators, because we use a number of computers in our work (classroom, library, computer lab, home, etc.). Under most conditions, these bookmarks cannot be carried from one computer to another. This problem has been solved by a number of Web-based bookmark services first introduced to educators by the education technology visionary, John Kuglin, when he delivered the keynote address at the National Educational Computing Conference in 2000. He brought the house down as he demonstrated Backflip.

Backflip is an online bookmarking service that stores your favorite Web sites in an online database, so that you can easily access them through the Web. As a result, teachers and learners can carry their personal digital libraries around with them, having access anytime and anyplace you have access to the World Wide Web.

Online bookmarking became even more interesting in the last few years, as the application has evolved into a genre of Web services called social bookmarks. Sites like FURL and Delicious utilize two new techniques that turn our bookmarks into massive collaborative digital libraries.

First, online bookmarks and other information organizers are abandoning the metaphor of *folders*, replacing it with *tags*. This means that instead of thinking about organizing information inside of a container, such as a folder, file cabinet, or book shelf, we place a tag on the information. One benefit of this scheme is the freedom to place any number of tags on a single Web site, photo, or other information, in effect, placing it into several categories. In addition, these tags can be searched in a way that collects Web sites (and other types of information) into dynamic groups—or folders, if you will, categorizations that literally form themselves in front of us.

As an example, my Delicious bookmarks include a tag for *blogtools*. Here I store Web sites about tools that assist bloggers and readers of blogs. When I click that tag, I can view all 23 of those Web sites. I also learn that, among those sites, are tags for 13 other topics, including: *21st century literacy*, *podcasting*, *data visualization,* and *Wikis*. Clicking those tags causes new groupings of Web sites.

Secondly, tagging becomes even more useful as these services use their databases to link through single usership, treating the services as a much larger collaborative library that users contribute to. For instance, if I have a number of Web sites stored in my Delicious site related to one of the units I teach

Web Resources

http://kuglin.com/
http://furl.net
http://delicious.com

in my U.S. History course, for instance, the Colonial Period of U.S. History, I might tag those sites with *colonialperiod*. Clicking that tag will cause those sites to form into a group.

To the right of each Web site is a blue tab with a number. This number indicates how many other people have also bookmarked that Web site. When I click the blue tab (79), the 79 other people who have bookmarked the site are listed. Next to each user is a list of tags they assigned to the site. Scanning down the list, I discover a user, whose login name is historyteacher52. It is reasonable to assume that the owner of that login is another history teacher. Next to the name is a list of tags that historyteacher52 applied, including prerevolution. When I click prerevolution, I see all of the sites that historyteacher52 has categorized as related to the years leading up to the American Revolutionary War, and many of the sites are new to me.

Bookmarks are becoming a social network, where people are not merely storing their favorite Web sites, but also contributing to a global library that is dynamically organized around tags. For instance, if we go to:

http://delicious.com/tag/greatdepression

we receive a list of Web sites that Delicious users have saved and tagged with the term *greatdepression*. Number four in the list is a Web site entitled *Photographs of the Great Depression*. The site appears on this list because others have found it to be useful. Again, it is content by recommendation.

We can also treat these services like a search engine. If I am planning a presentation on scientific visualization, I might go to the Delicious home page and enter *visualization* in the search box. I receive a list of Web sites saved by Delicious users that were tagged with visualization or included the term in the title or description. These are Web sites that other people have found to be valuable enough to save. The first four sites in the list have each been bookmarked by more than 5,000 users. Once again, content by recommendation.

Goochland County Public Schools, Virginia, has a social bookmark environment for the entire school system. To make it easier for teachers to find valuable Web resources, they contribute together to a single account, which all of the professional staff can access. Their tags include subjects (art, biology, civics, English), information literacy (copyright), and even tags for the levels of the Virginia Standards of Learning, or SOLs. As teachers identify new sites in their research or casual Web surfings, and add them to the district's Delicious site, the sites become accessible to all other teachers in the district and to us (Dembo).

Since Delicious is an open Web service, it is probably not appropriate for student use, except through RSS feeds. Tim Lauer, principal of the Lewis Elementary School in Portland, Oregon, wanted his young students to be able to organize and contribute to their own digital libraries, to make it easier to

Web Resource

http://sourceforge.net/projects/scuttle/

find Web-based information resources. However, using one of the open tools like Furl or Delicious presented a possibility that his students might click through to content that was inappropriate. Lauer located an open source project called de.lirio.us (now Scuttle), which is social bookmarking software that can be downloaded and installed on a school or district Web server. Running social bookmarks independent of one of the worldwide services dramatically reduces the risks (Lauer).

Investigative Strategies—Finding Witnesses

Global information is **connected** in ways that it has never been in the past. Most of the billions of online documents available over the Internet are connected to other documents, which are connected to others, forming a global Web of information—an information universe. Finding information within this universe that helps you accomplish your goal is often a challenge. It sometimes involves a process of investigation, of detective work, more than mere technical practice. True Internet researchers are detectives, investigating a digital universe for answers and solutions. Much like the criminal detective, they search for clues, find and organize evidence, and make a case.

When detectives pursue their investigations, they are just as interested in witnesses as they are in physical evidence. This is why it is important not to overlook the people on the Internet who might help with our information needs. We typically think of Web pages when we go to the Net for the answer to a question. But often it is the people who can provide the most valuable information.

Community

The parents of our students can be a good first place to look for digital witnesses. They are an underutilized resource because of busy schedules. However, one of the most important benefits of wiring our schools is the conduit that forms between our classrooms and libraries, and the homes of our students. A parent whose profession, hobby, or travel experience might enhance your next unit is suddenly reachable through e-mail, instant messaging, or even Web-based teleconferencing.

Get to know who your students' parents are. "It takes a village . . .", but we have to invite that village in. Use Figure 2.4 as a model for collecting information on potential Internet guest speakers during next year's open house or on an ongoing basis. It is also available as an editable file on this book's Web site.

Johnston Jones Middle School
Volunteer Form

Parent Name: _____   Student Name: _____

Parent Phone Number: _____
Parent E-mail Address: _____
IM Network & Screen Name: _____

Outline of Topics Covered This Year
Please check any topics with which you might be prepared to contribute.

Sept	Ecosystems	[ ]	Feb	Landforms	[ ]
Nov	Energy	[ ]	Apr	Weather & Climate	[ ]

I can interact with class by:		I can provide:	
Visiting the class	[ ]	Personal information	[ ]
Speaker Phone	[ ]	Photos	[ ]
E-mail	[ ]	Computer Slideshow	[ ]
Chat	[ ]	Video	[ ]
Video conference	[ ]	Access to other experts	[ ]

_____
signed

Figure 2.4: Volunteer Form

Another strategy for locating potential virtual speakers for your classroom is to find a Web site that includes the information that you are teaching, presented in a way that is consistent with the way that you teach it. Then, rather than (or in addition to) having students use the site, invite the Web master or author of the site to contribute to your lesson in some more direct way through e-mail, instant messenger, or video conferencing.

Web Resource

http://davidwarlick.com/redefining_literacy

Mailing Lists

Mailing lists (See Figure 2.5: Mailing Lists) are another potent source for experts, whom you can invite into your classroom. As an example, let's assume that you are a health teacher looking for ways to convey to your students the importance of healthful living habits. It might be beneficial to find an online community of experts on nutrition or exercise and then use them as a resource for your students. However, be open to the idea that experts do not always come with credentials. Sometimes, the best expertise comes from experience; in this case, maybe that expertise comes from people who are suffering from their poor habits of the past.

Internet Mailing List

Through the Internet people with similar interests and needs can create online communities where they can compare, share, inform, and develop ideas related to their mutual pursuits.

Technically, a mailing list is a list of e-mail addresses belonging to the members of the community. When one member sends a message to the list, copies of the message are automatically sent to all other members. When another member replies to the message, copies of the response are also sent out to all members.

The members of the list experience a group discussion through which problems are solved, questions are answered, and information is shared.

A hard disk somewhere on the Internet

E-mail addresses of list members

1 One member posts a question.

2. All members receive a copy of the message.

3. Another member answers the question and all other members receive the answer.

Figure 2.5: Mailing Lists

One of the possible outcomes of poor health habits is heart disease. There may be a mailing list that is devoted to group support among people with heart disease, where they can share their experiences, problems, solutions, latest research, and other information that is mutually beneficial to the group. Might these people have something to share with your students? How might we locate such a group?

There are thousands of mailing lists on the Internet covering just about any topic that you could imagine, and many that you could not imagine. There are also a number of tools that can help you find mailing lists that discuss the topic you are looking for. We might try a tool called *Catalist* first. Catalist is like other search engines except that it searches for mailing lists instead of Web pages. It specifically searches for mailing lists that use the *Listserv* mailing list management software, a product of L-Soft, which also owns Catalist. It is important to note that Listserv is a highly sophisticated product that requires a fairly high degree of technical expertise to install and maintain.

Web Resource

http://lsoft.com/lists/list_q.html

This is important because only organizations that can afford this level of expertise typically use Listserv (corporations, universities, hospitals, established non-profits), implying that these might be more serious mailing lists.

You visit **Catalist** and enter the key term *heart disease* into the search box. After a moment one mailing list appears, entitled Congenital Heart Disease. If you are unsure about the definition of *congenital*, you quickly access an online dictionary from your personal digital library and look it up, discovering that it means, "existing at or dating from birth," or you might go to Google and type "define: congenital." Google delivers 26 definitions in English from various Web sources, and six definitions in French. But the meaning is the same—a disease, deformity, or deficiency existing at the time of birth. You decide that this list is not related to your search for problems resulting from bad health practices.

Our problem is that the hits, or resulting list of finds, are too narrow. We need to broaden our scope to include more possible online communities to choose from. So we simplify our search term. Rather than entering *heart disease*, we shorten it to just *heart*.

This time Catalist delivers 35 hits on a wider range of topics, some of which have nothing to do with health. But, from the descriptions that we receive, we learn that a number of the mailing lists are related to heart diseases and those who suffer from them. We select one of these lists, click the title, and learn some basic information including the number of members of this list, how to reach the list archive, and instructions for joining the list. By clicking the Web **Archive Interface** link, we get a search tool that enables us to browse through messages that have already been posted by the members week by week, or enter a search term to access all messages that include that word or phrase. Entering the word *diet* returns hundreds of messages, each a possible source of information for your students.

To join the list, you are provided with an e-mail address and a join command. You simply start an e-mail message to the address provided, and paste the command (usually *subscribe [list name]*) into the body of the message. After sending the message, you receive a reply from the mailing list computer either welcoming you to the list or giving further instructions for confirming your registration.

In most cases, you would go ahead and join the list and start receiving copies of all of the messages posted by its members. However, the issues here are somewhat sensitive and personal. So it would be wise to seek permission from the owner of the list first. His or her e-mail address is also provided. Figure 2.6 provides an example of how such a message might be written.

```
            To: owner@listserv.mich.edu
            Cc:
           Bcc:
       Subject: Inquiry on Diet Mailing List

       Dear List Owner,

       I am a 6th grade health teacher in North Carolina.  Part of my curriculum is to
       convey to my students the importance of a healthy diet and exercise.  I would like
       to join your [list name] mailing list for a three-week period and monitor the
       discussions for tips, advice, and other information that may be especially
       convincing to my students.

       Further, with your permission, I would like to post up three questions to the list
       seeking out advice from heart patients that may effectively impress on my 6th
       grade students how critical it is to take care of their health.

       I look forward to your reply.

       Regards,

       Janice Sneedley
       Health Teacher, Johnson Middle School
       Johnson, NC
       <http://xsd.k12.nc.us/sneedley5>
       jsneedley@xsd.k12.nc.us
```

Figure 2.6: E-Mail

Notice that this message is short, to the point, and describes clearly why you want to join the list and what you intend to do. Other mailing list search tools include:

- Nextmark,
- Tile.Net, and
- The Linguist List.

The Blogosphere

The Internet has erupted with new opportunities for people to share their expertise, specifically through their blogs and podcasts. We have already explored blogging as one dimension into which people are expressing themselves. Blogs can be an even richer source of witnesses than mailing lists. People who share their job topics, hobbies, or travel interest through blogs demonstrate a willingness to not only talk about the subjects that they care about, but also to publish it in a more formal way.

It is easy to find blogging experts through a number of search engines that focus on blog sites. Google, for example, provides a blog search feature. A search for *heart disease* returned more than one and a quarter million blog posts mentioning the term.

Web Resource

http://nextmark.com/
http://tile.net/lists/
http://listserv.linguistlist.org:8080/mls/html/
http://blogsearch.google.com/

We have talked about Technorati, which indexes more than 112 million bloggers. Searching for *heart disease* in Technorati returns more than 250,000 posts. But Technorati provides some fine-tuning that other blog search engines do not. The 250,000 posts listed merely mention the term. Some are serious examinations of the topic and potentially point to valuable witness sources. However, many are not experts, such as a college student who is blogging about an aunt who was just diagnosed with arteriosclerosis.

In addition to searching for blog posts, Technorati also enables us to search for bloggers who have included the term *heart disease* in the description of their blog. This search returns 512 bloggers who are explicitly writing about some aspect of heart disorders. Visiting and reading some of these blogs will reveal those who are most appropriate to provide support to your class. It is also worth noting that Technorati attempts to calculate a level of authority for the bloggers that turn up in its searches. This authority index, like Google, is based on the number of other bloggers who link to the listed blog site. Our listing of blogs about heart disease is headed *by Jimmy Moore's Livin' La Vida Low-Carb™ Blog*, with an authority index of 432. Its rank is 12,423, which means that 12,423 other blogs are linked to more than La Vida Low-Carb. Out of more than 112 million bloggers, this is a pretty good ranking.

Although useful, it is important not to put complete faith in this form of ranking by recommendation. A previous search for blog articles mentioning *education* that was topped off by three bloggers with rankings of more than 2,000 also included the "Flying Spaghetti Monster," a parody religion whose beliefs are known as Pastafarianism.
Other blogging search tools include:

- Blogpulse,
- Icerocket,
- Blogscope, and
- Bloglines.

Web Resources

http://blogpulse.com/
http://icerocket.com/
http://blogscope.net/
http://bloglines.com/
http://google.com/
http://podcastalley.com/
http://podcastdirectory.com/
http://epnweb.org/

Podcasts can be another source of expertise. You can find numerous podcasts on a variety of subjects using the iTunes Store within the iTunes application for both Mac OS and Windows. Other podcast directors include:

- Podcast Alley,
- Podcast Directory, and
- The Education Podcast Network.

Investigative Strategies—Finding Evidence

Search Engines, such as Google and Yahoo, are powerful and immensely valuable tools that enable us to search for information through enormous online collections, sifting through billions of Web documents for specific words and phrases. With these seemingly magical tools at our disposal, it is important to understand exactly what is happening when we use a search engine to seek Web pages on a given topic.

First of all, search engines do not search the Internet, at least in the way that you might suspect. When searching a book for the answer to your question, you rarely scan the entire book. You scan the table of contents or index for references to the problem. Search engines also search indexes to find references to related Web pages. These indexes can be huge, holding references to billions of Web documents, as is the case with **Google**. The indexes of other search engines can be small. Yahoo's directory index represents only a tiny fraction of what Google holds. However, this does not mean that Google's search index is better than Yahoo's directory. It means that they enable us to solve different kinds of problems. Sometimes it is more suitable to deal with 200 hits than with 400,000 hits.

It is also helpful to understand that most search engines create their own indexes. If we had to rely on people to add all of the Web pages to a search engine's index, we would be woefully behind in representing the content of the World Wide Web in our searches. These enormous indexes are grown and maintained by semi-intelligent software agents.

> **The true intelligence of the World Wide Web is between your ears.**

Before your imagination starts to produce electronic snoopers crawling a global web of wires, let me explain that these agents, often called spiders, are merely small pieces of software that are programmed to wander through the World Wide Web, following hyperlinks in much the same way that you browse through links as you surf the Net. These spider programs record the links that they encounter, and when they find a link that has not been recorded, they follow it to its target page. The spider then checks the page to see if it is already known by the search engine. If not, the spider sends all of the pertinent information about the page back to the search engine, where it is added to the index. This is automatic and continual, and an essential part of what makes the Web so useful.

This is an important concept to understand, because it explains why, when you use a search engine, you often receive a large number of hits that seem to be completely unrelated to your topic. Search engines are wonderfully powerful tools, but they cannot think. They search for strings of characters, not meaning. They do the best that they can to put the most relevant pages at the top of your list of hits, but they do not truly understand what you want. The true intelligence of the World Wide Web is between your ears.

Examining the sites, comparing the meaning of information, and making judgments and decisions about the value of the information is still the job of people. It is a skill that we learn by doing and sharing with others—and becoming responsible for our work. Net research is something that educators should be doing every day, continually building your skills, building your knowledge and teaching resources in your personal digital library, and sharing with appropriate colleagues what you have found. We should be modeling this behavior in front of our students.

In 2003, only 7 to 8 percent of Web destinations were reached using a search engine. According to a Search Engine Watch report, *Direct Navigation to Sites Rules, But Search Engines Remain Important*, 52 percent were reached by entering the URL and 41 percent by clicking links (Sullivan). This report has not been updated, but the following listing of the top 10 Web destinations indicates a great usage of search engines compared to five years ago.

Alexa ("Top Sites by Country"), a company that measures Internet usage by tracking Web traffic, listed the following top 10 Web sites by traffic.

1. Yahoo!—http://yahoo.com/

2. Google—http://.google.com/

3. YouTube—http://youtube.com/

4. Windows Live—http://live.com/

5. Microsoft Network (MSN)—http://msn.com/

6. MySpace—http://myspace.com/

7. Wikipedia—http://wikipedia.org/

8. Facebook—http://facebook.com/

9. Blogger.com—http://blogger.com/

10. Yahoo! Japan—http://yahoo.co.jp/

Of the 10 Web sites listed, four are search engines, five connect us to people and their work (social networks and social media), and the remaining site, Wikipedia, is entirely about finding information.

Most of the readers of this book have used search engines to find information on the Internet. You have typed keywords into your favorite search engine and then scanned through the first 20 or 30 Web pages out of the tens of thousands (or millions) of hits. Or you may simply settle for one of the first five or six pages that appear in the list. Some of you may have even been improving your results by using Boolean or search math to refine your search phrases. Search strategy, however, is far deeper than knowing when to use AND, OR, and NOT.

Let us consider a scenario, a middle school student conducting Internet research in order to complete an assignment. Her name is Suzette, and her teacher has given her class the following assignment.

> It is 2050 and we are terraforming the planet Mars. Scientists are identifying animals from our planet to migrate to Mars and are especially interested in grazing animals. Your assignment is to select a grazing animal and submit a report that describes the animal and how it interacts with other organisms in its ecosystem.

Suzette has two problems:

1.   Select a grazing animal for her report.

2.   Collect information about the animal and how it interacts with other organisms.

She starts, as most of us do, with a large index search engine such as Google, entering *grazing animals* as her search term. Suzette receives 280,000 hits. She scans the first page or two of hits, discovering Web sites on grazing terminology, official documents from the U.S. Environmental Protection Agency, and books on the management of domestic farm animals in The Netherlands. Although some of these pages might be helpful later, they do not help Suzette with her first problem, selecting a grazing animal.

Our student researcher then decides that she needs Web pages that have more general information on grazing animals. So she decides to use Yahoo. Although this search tool contains a powerful search engine, Suzette decides to use its Web directory. The difference between a Web directory and search engine is that the directory stores what it knows about the Internet by subject, topic, and subtopic. You start with a page of general subjects (Business, Computers, News, Arts, Reference, and more) and select the subject that comes closest to solving your problem. This produces a list of topics that belong to your selected subject. Clicking the appropriate topic usually produces a list of subtopics. The benefit is that the final list of Web sites is short and the sites are typically of a more general nature.

Suzette selects **Science** as the initial subject and then **Animals, Insects, & Pets** from the following list of topics. Among the subtopics that appear, Suzette selects **Mammals**, because most of the grazing animals she knows of have hair and bear their young alive. However, the following list of subtopics does not include grazing mammals, nor does it include links that might help identify grazing animals. Our student researcher rethinks again, deciding that she needs to go even more general, seeking a site that includes all animals. Such a site might have information to help her select only grazing animals.

Suzette backs out from the **Mammals** page to **Animals, Insects, & Pets**. She scrolls down to the listing of Web sites on the page (Yahoo directory pages list subtopics of the preceding topic and then links to Web sites that are appropriate) and selects Animal Diversity Web because it probably has information about the animals that will help her solve her first problem.

From this Web site, she can select animals by class (e.g. mammals, birds, amphibians) and subclass (e.g. prototheria, metatheria, eutheria). Again, not very helpful, but this detail of information indicates a fairly rich Web site. So she switches strategy, again returning to Google. Here she enters *grazing* into the search box followed by *site:animaldiversity.ummz.umich.edu*. By adding the word *site* followed by a colon and the Web address of Animal Diversity Web, Google will search for pages with *grazing* only within the *www.animaldiversity.ummz.umich.edu* site. This was an especially good strategy because not only did Google report pages on grazing animals, but also animals that are affected by grazing animals. This will be helpful in solving her second problem as well.

As Suzette reviews a number of the grazing animals, she discovers that certain birds, fish, and mollusks are also considered grazers. This idea challenges her previous perception of grazing animals, enriching the concept in her mind. This is a good and useful byproduct of searching the Internet. You nearly always learn something new.

Suzette selects the Saiga Antelope partly because it is so ugly it is cute, but mostly because it lives in an ecosystem that is in flux. Its habitat was closely regulated by the Soviet Union. However, after the nations of that former state separated, the smaller, less wealthy individual countries could not enforce regulations and the antelope came under attack by poachers, was affected by the decline of predators, and came into more frequent contact with domestic grazing animals, causing the spread of disease.

Suzette continues her research by entering *saiga* and *antelope* into Google. She receives over a thousand hits and she realizes that these are pages that have *saiga* somewhere and *antelope* somewhere, not necessarily together. She adjusts her search to *"saiga antelope."* The quotation marks force Google to find only pages that include the phrase *saiga antelope*, the two words together. This decreases the number of hits to only 882.

Our student researcher begins scanning the pages, finding a great deal of information about the Saiga, and also a couple of sites about the animal's environment, each of which includes the word *ecosystem*. There are other pages mixed in, especially advertisements for books about animals. She feels that what she needs is among the 882 Web pages, but rather than waste time continuing to scan this many pages, she decides to refine her search one more time:

This final search phrase asks for pages that have the term or phrase *saiga antelope* and also the word *ecosystem* somewhere on the page. It will, however, omit any pages that have the word *book*. This is signaled by the minus sign in front of the word *book*. The result is 102 hits with just the information she seeks.

Searching the Internet is a process. It is an investigation, an act of finding clues and evidence and refining your strategy based on those clues. I hope that the scenario above has helped you to understand this process and to understand how this process can be instructional on its own. Because we are using information to navigate the Internet, each adaptation of our search strategy leads to a new understanding of the topic and the knowledge that surrounds it.

Another way to teach the search process is to use a model called S.E.A.R.C.H. This is an acronym that represents the steps of using a process approach to searching the Net. (See Figure 2.7: Search)

Start	Small and Simple. It may not be helpful to start with Google, which could deliver millions of hits on the first search. Start with a small indexed search engine, such as Yahoo. Examine a sampling of hits indentifying words common in the relevant resources and words common in the less than relevant pages.
Edit	Use the words identified in the previous step to Edit your search phrase. Use Boolean or Search Math as the grammar of your search phrase.
Advance	Advance to a large database search engine, such as Google. Enter the Edited search phrase and examine a sampling of hits, identifying more words that are common in pages that help you solve your problem and pages that are not relevant.
Refine	Refine your search phrase using the words identified in your Advance search.
Cycle	Cycle back and advance again.
Harvest	Harvest the resources that were identified during your searches. This is an ongoing process.

Figure 2.7: Search

At the heart of the process is the continuing cycle of searching (See Figure 2.8: Search Cycle), examining the information, looking for clues and evidence, refining the search strategy, and searching again. With each pass, you learn more about the topic. You also become exposed to different types of information. You may have expected general Web pages, but encountered tabular data describing the topic or images. You may even find video and sound files or even virtual reality files. Each of these unexpected types of information will enrich your knowledge about the topic at hand.

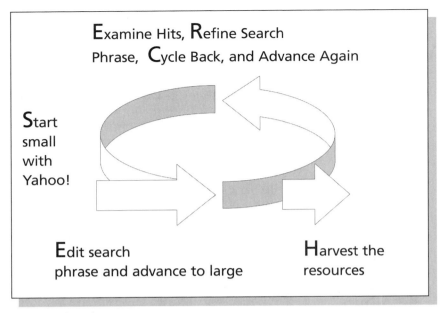

Examine Hits, Refine Search
Phrase, Cycle Back, and Advance Again

Start
small
with
Yahoo!

Edit search
phrase and advance to large

Harvest the
resources

Figure 2.8: Search Cycle

Investigative Strategies—Search Logs

As students are conducting their research, it is important that they think about their target, what they are finding, and how they are adjusting their search strategies. One way of assuring that they think about their search is to ask them to keep a search log. Maintaining a search log will make the search process more tedious, but having students write down their evolving strategies will help them to see it as exactly that, an evolving and growing strategy. A search log should ask students to identify the goal of their research and the initial search term or phrase. Then with each search, they should record the words that they find to be common in useful Web pages that appear (attractors) and words that are common in pages that are not useful (rejectors). Then the student researcher should record the refinements that they make to their search phrase. In addition to causing students to think more about their search strategies, keeping a search log also enables them to look back at their developing strategies and retry alternative phrases. Above is the log that Suzette kept (See Figure 2.9: Search Evaluation), as she conducted her research on grazing animals. A blank version of this log form is available on the book's Web site.

Finally, search logs can easily be kept on paper. However, it makes much more sense if students can complete them digitally as a word processing file. It saves time, because students are able to copy and paste words and terms, rather than writing them on paper. In addition, they can edit their evolving search phrases more easily with the word processor and then copy and paste the text directly

Internet Search Evaluation Tool

Search Tool	Search Phrase
[ ] Yahoo [ ] Alta Vista [x] Google [ ] Yahooligans [ ] Lycos Other:	*grazing animals*
Comments: *Received more than 280,000 hits, and most of the first ones were too specific. Will try for a more general search using Yahoo.*	
[X] Yahoo [ ] Alta Vista [ ] Google [ ] Yahooligans [ ] Lycos Other:	*Science/Animals, Insects, & Pets/Mammals*
Comments: *No subtopics for grazing animals. Must broaden search by dropping back out to all animals*	
[X] Yahoo [ ] Alta Vista [ ] Google [ ] Yahooligans [ ] Lycos Other:	*Science/Animals, Insects, & Pets*
Comments: *Found page with information about animals and how they are different. Should have information about grazing animals. Animal Diversity Web.*	
[ ] Yahoo [ ] Alta Vista [X] Google [ ] Yahooligans [ ] Lycos Other:	*grazing site:animaldiversity.ummz.umich.edu*
Comments: *Received 117 pages in Animal Diversity with the word grazing. Very good information. Selecting Saiga Antelope.*	
[ ] Yahoo [ ] Alta Vista [X] Google [ ] Yahooligans [ ] Lycos Other:	*saiga antelope*
Comments: *1,360 hits. Not many useful in first few pages. New strategy.*	
[ ] Yahoo [X] Alta Vista [ ] Google [ ] Yahooligans [ ] Lycos Other:	*"saiga antelope"*
Comments: *Down to 882 hits. Many pages about Saiga. Also many pages about book about saiga. Found one page with information about ecosystem. New strategy.*	
[ ] Yahoo [X] Alta Vista [ ] Google [ ] Yahooligans [ ] Lycos Other:	*"saiga antelope" ecosystem —book*
Comments: *Down to 102 hits. Pages about saiga environment and ecosystem. Bingo!*	

Figure 2.9: Search Evaluation

into the search engine. Anything that can be done to ease the labor of conducting research will improve the success of the task.

Investigative Strategies—Search Language

Some readers may have been involved in computers and education long enough to remember *Dialog*. This was one of the earliest online information services and was used in many school libraries. The problem with Dialog was that it charged by the minute, and the fees were substantial. As a result, the process for searching their database involved spending time composing, editing, and refining your search phrase before even touching the computer.

After assuring that your search phrase was complete, you dialed up, logged in, typed in your search phrase, received the list of hits, printed them out, and logged out as quickly as you could. This provided schools with access to information that was not available otherwise, but it was not a good model for the kind of research we conduct today. With the Internet, research is a more interactive process, where you begin with a simple strategy and increasingly refine your search phrase based on what you find and learn.

This interaction requires that we communicate with the search tool in order to define what we are looking for using a language that the search engine understands. With Dialog (and some Internet search engines today) the language for posing our search questions is called Boolean. This powerful set of rules and syntax enables you to describe the information you want and how it relates to other information. For instance, you are looking for information about Native Americans in the state of Ohio. You decide what words will probably appear in the Web pages that hold your information and enter those words. As an example, you might enter the following search phrase:

native americans indians ohio

The result is Web pages about native everything, American patriotism, all things Indian, everything you could imagine about the state of Ohio, and a slew of Web pages about the Cleveland Indians baseball team—about five million hits on Google. You clearly need to refine your search phrase (strategy), and you do this by describing the relation between these bits of information.

For instance, *native* and *americans* must be together as a phrase in order to have the meaning we are looking for. So we put quotation marks around this phrase.

"native americans" indians ohio

We know that sometimes the reference will be to *native americans* and sometimes it will be *indians*. So we insert a connector between the two words, *OR* (all caps).
"native americans" OR indians ohio
Searching for Native Americans or Indians is a separate issue from the state. So that sub-phrase is placed in parentheses and *ohio* is connected with an *AND*, indicating that it must be a part of the pages that are reported.

("native americans" OR indians) AND ohio

Finally, to remove references to the baseball team, we add a *NOT* connector and the phrase *Cleveland Indians* in quotation marks.

("native americans" OR indians) AND ohio NOT "cleveland indians"

The results are Web pages that mention *Native Americans* or *Indians* along with *Ohio*, but do not mention the *Cleveland Indians* ball team—about 13,000 hits.

In review, Boolean uses the following conventions:

- Quotation marks around phrases that have unique meaning,

- AND separating terms that must both appear in the returned Web pages,

- OR separating terms that either of which must appear in the returned pages,

- NOT preceding words or terms that must not appear in the returned pages.

Although this might seem complicated, it is not. Boolean is, however, difficult to explain, and for this reason, most Internet search engines have switched to a language called *Search Math*. It is not quite as powerful as Boolean, but search math is much easier to explain. In Search Math,

- All connectors are assumed to be AND.

- Phrases are created with quotation marks, in the same way as Boolean.

- Some of the search engines will accept OR as a connector.

- If there is a word or phrase that should not appear in the search, then it is preceded by a minus symbol (-) with no space between.

The Boolean phrase that we constructed above would be entered in search math as:

"native americans" OR indians +ohio -"cleveland indians"

Each search engine has its own set of conventions for composing your search phrase, and they change frequently. For this reason, I will not report them here. However, Greg Notess keeps an up-to-date chart listing the features of individual search engines on his Web site, Search Engine Showdown.

Thus far, we have only sought out Web pages with most any type of information. There are lots of search tools, and many of them search for specific types of information. Following is a list of various search tools arrange by their specialty.

Web Resource

http://searchengineshowdown.com/features/

Search Tools

General Search Engines

Google—http://google.com/

Alta Vista—http://altavista.com/

All The Web (FAST)—http://alltheweb.com/

Yahoo—http://yahoo.com/

Lycos—http://lycos.com/

Ask—http://ask.com/

News Search Engines

Google News—http://news.google.com/

Alta Vista News—http://news.altavista.com/

Yahoo News—http://news.yahoo.com/

Ananova—http://ananova.com/

Crayon—http://crayon.net/

World News Network—http://wn.com/

Multimedia Search Engines

Google Images—http://images.google.com/

Google Video—http://video.google.com/

Lycos Pictures & Sound—http://multimedia.lycos.com/

Flickr—http://flickr.com/

FAST—http://multimedia.alltheweb.com/

Ditto—http://ditto.com/

Metacrawlers & Meta Search Engines

Ixquick—http://ixquick.com/

Vivisimo—http://vivisimo.com/

Kartoo—http://kartoo.com/

Kid-Friendly Search Tools

Ask Jeeves for Kids—http://ajkids.com/

Yahoo Kids—http://kids.yahoo.com/

KidsClick!—http://kidsclick.com/

Investigative Strategies—RSS (Training the Information to Find You)

The job of libraries is to give us a place to find information. They shop for, select, and buy books, and they evaluate and subscribe to magazines, journals, and online databases. They select valuable sources of content and streams of ideas that will be useful to their patrons, organize that information so that we can find what we need, and help us with the skills required to navigate and evaluate that information. We also go to our own set of encyclopedias to find information. We go to Google to find information. Yet, something new, potent, and more than a little strange has happened in this new information landscape that is changing a lot about how we use information.

It started with a problem that was rendering the blogging community almost useless. If you are reading eight education bloggers, you are probably challenged to find time and routine to visit those eight blog pages every day to check for new articles. Unfortunately, many people did not have the discipline to visit all of those Web pages everyday for new content. It is not our work style, nor is it an easy routine for many people to make a part of their everyday information experience.

Then came Dave Winer, a Berkley software developer, who refined and brought into the blogging community a protocol designed for syndicating content. Initiated by Netscape and later dropped, Winer adopted the protocol for the publishing software that his company, UserLand Software, was producing—including blogging software. Winer named the protocol, *RSS*, short for *Rich Site Summary* (*Really Simple Syndication* is easier to remember).

How RSS Works

Each time a blogger adds a new article, her blogging software, e.g. Wordpress, generates two versions of that blog page. One is the blog page that human readers see. It is public and we can read it by going to the blog home page. At the same time, the software generates another file, an RSS feed, which is written to be read by a computer, not people. RSS feeds are written in a language called XML, short for Extensible Markup Language (about as geeky as this book is going to get).

Figure 2.10 illustrates the two versions of my blog content. The first, *human readable* version, is formatted to be viewed on a standard Web browser and easi-

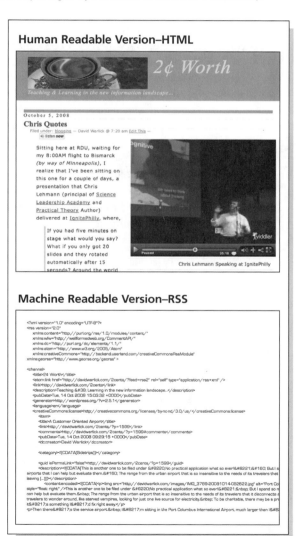

Figure 2.10: HTML-RSS

ly read by people. It is formatted with short paragraphs, bulleted lists, graphs, and photographs where they enhance the message.

The second version, *machine readable*, is obviously not intended for human consumption. It is computer code that is intended to provide, for the computer, information about the information that is available for reading—metadata, or data about the data. The RSS feed includes nearly all of the content that is available to human readers. It also includes information about the information that computers can use to work the information in a variety of ways.

One more element needs to be added for all of this to make sense within the context of contemporary literacy. **Feed aggregators** are software programs or Web applications that are designed to read RSS feeds. They are configured to periodically access the URL address of RSS feed files of the blogs that the aggregator's owner is following and then inform the owner of new content, and sometimes even display the content of the blog inside the aggregator. As a result, the reader merely checks his feed aggregator to access information from all of the blogs he is paying attention to or has subscribed to with the aggregator.

If this sounds complicated, it is only because you've probably never done anything like this with a computer before. To some degree, it's like subscribing to a newspaper or a magazine, but there are several dimensions to using RSS that cannot be compared to the print world, or anything else. So let's look at an example.

One of the first and most popular aggregators was a Web-based tool called **Bloglines**. After you have established an account on Bloglines *(click **Register** on the opening page)*, you login and click the feeds tab near the top of the page. This reveals a panel to the left of the page that lists the blogs that you have subscribed to already—at this point, none. You are now ready to start adding RSS feeds.

A librarian friend of yours has suggested a blog to you, Joyce Valenza's **Neverending Search Blog**. You visit the page and decide that Joyce is an educator-librarian you should pay attention to.

To the right of the title of her blog, you see an orange symbol—the first item in Figure 2.11. These logos or symbols all represent RSS feeds, and are usually hyperlinks to the RSS file.

Figure 2.11: RSS Buttons

Your aggregator needs the location, or URL address, of the RSS feed for Valenza's blog. To capture this, you right click on the link, the RSS symbol, and then select **Copy Link Location** *(FireFox)* or **Copy Shortcut** *(Internet Explorer)*. This temporarily places the URL or Internet address of the RSS feed in the memory of the computer.

Now we return to your Bloglines page and click the **Add** link at the top left of the page. This click produces a textbox in the middle of the larger right panel, labeled *Blog* or *Feed URL*. Paste the RSS Feed address you just copied from Valenza's blog page into the textbox, and then click the **Subscribe** button.

You receive a number of options for the feed. The default settings are appropriate for most applications, so just click the **Subscribe** button again at the bottom of the page again.

Joyce Valenza's blog appears in the left panel, with a number to the right or beneath the blog. If the number is 10, then there are 10 blog entries that Joyce has written in the last two weeks that you have not read. When you click the title of her blog, all 10 entries appear in the larger panel on the right, where you can read them. You can also click the title of a specific blog entry to load the original blog.

As you add new blogs that you learn of, and delete blogs that become less useful, you are growing a library of educator voices that you can cultivate to help you do your job. Each time you load your Bloglines page, it goes out, checks the RSS feeds of the bloggers you have subscribed to, and then informs you of the number of blog entries that have been added that you have not read yet.

Figure 2.12 illustrates the classic layout of most common RSS Feed aggregators, listing the blogs subscribed to on the left and using the larger panel to

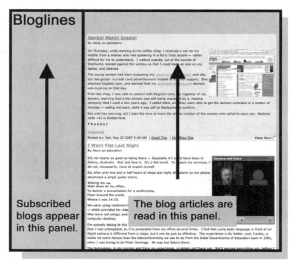

Figure 2.12: Aggregator Layout

the right for the content. Most browsers now include RSS aggregation, as well, making RSS reading an internal part of your information browsing experience.

Start Pages are also gaining in popularity, especially among educators, as RSS aggregators. Yahoo and Google both offer start page tools for users, each including the ability to subscribe to RSS feeds. Two other start pages that are used by many educators are **Pageflakes, Netvibes,** and **iGoogle**. Blogs are subscribed to in much the same way as Bloglines and others, but the layout is different. It is almost completely customizable. Subscribed blogs appear as modules on the page that can be dragged around and repositioned as you need. You can create what looks like a newspaper, with content from bloggers coming to you. It becomes your personal digital newspaper, for which you are the editor, selecting the content that will be printed and the layout of the pages.

Figure 2.13 illustrates a generic start page style aggregator. The tabs at the top click to various pages in the aggregator, listing education sources, news sources, technology, media, and entertainment sources. Each box on the page represents a different blog or other RSS feed. The boxes can be picked up and moved with your mouse, so that you can arrange your feeds in a way that makes them easier to use. For instance, you may have a reason to have your local bloggers in one column and international bloggers in another. You can customize how many of the latest articles will appear in each box and customize other configurations.

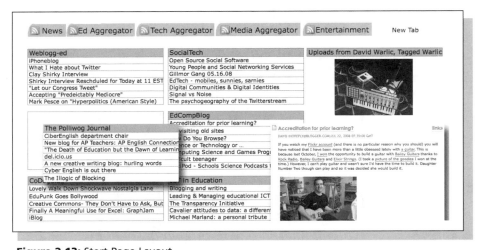

Figure 2.13: Start Page Layout

It is important to remember that your aggregator is personal. It is designed to be constantly cultivated and pruned, depending on your ongoing needs and challenges.

Investigative Strategy—Evaluating the Information

Our use of information has experienced a significant and important shift, and it has occurred almost un-noticed, especially in the prevailing conversations about curriculum over the past decade. It began with whispers, during the early days of the Internet, where scientists and scholars started to engage in professional conversations online, sharing data, ideas, insights, and publications over the Internet. Although collaboration did happen before that time, scholarly discourse occurred largely though juried publications, in an effort to assure the value of content. But the free flow of ideas and information moved to a new level with the Internet and the World Wide Web, and as the rise of HTML editors enabled anyone with any technical orientation and the funds to purchase or rent Web space to publish their ideas to a global audience.

This shift from broadcast, authority assuring information distribution mode, to a multicast, free flow of ideas mode, went into overdrive with the launch of Blogger in 1999, and the rapid growth of innovative new Web applications that expanded the Internet beyond a place for finding information, to a platform for knowledge-growing conversations—generating content that is indexed and available for future research. We've moved from being mere consumers of information to producers. We are becoming information artisans.

We have moved from an information monarchy to an environment that respects the wisdom and value of its readership. It is important to note that in the span of human history, this feudal, authority-based approach to information sharing is fairly recent. Throughout most of human history, information was shared around campfires, in the market place, or on the town square. Gutenberg's printing press changed things with the production of relatively cheap books, causing an enormous increase in the publishing of knowledge and stories and a globalization of ideas. It also created a historically unique relationship between content producers and content consumers.

One of the qualities of this relationship was the fact that our information was highly filtered, protecting us from extreme or fringe ideas. With notable exceptions, media were aimed at a common denominator of reader in order to garner the most consumers and revenue. Information came in containers (books and

Web Resource

http://blogger.com/

pamphlets), which themselves could be held in containers (libraries). Publishers and librarians controlled the information, protecting us from ideas that were counter-productive or harmful.

This layer of filtering provided by publishers of textbooks and other educational materials has helped teachers, by cushioning us from content that is not consistent with the established curriculum/standards. Being relieved from the responsibilities of evaluating and selecting content for instruction made our jobs easier. The information was produced and packaged for us. All we had to do was to teach it, and teach our children to read and believe it. We did not question it, and, as a result, we taught our children not to question it.

Today, the relationship between information producer and consumer is changing. Any of us can be content producers and distributors, and through our local bookmarks, online social bookmarking services, and our RSS aggregators, we are all becoming our own librarians. At the same time that this is providing unprecedented freedom of expression and wealth of content and perspective, it is also threatening the comfort of being able to teach and learn from reliable information sources. So how do we learn to be our own librarians? Who's going to teach us how to organize and add value to our personal digital libraries?

> **Sadly, there remain librarians who stand stalwartly at the gates guarding the information, seemingly oblivious to the fact that the walls and fences are gone.**

As publishing becomes free and the filtering agents we once depended on become less relevant to today's information landscape, we are left with a choice. Do we ignore the new, more engaged information landscape and keep teaching the way we always have, or do we pay attention and adapt to an information experience that will certainly be a part of the future for which we are preparing our children?

Sadly, there remain librarians who stand stalwartly at the gates guarding the information, seemingly oblivious to the fact that the walls and fences are gone. The information flows freely now, and we must come to understand that gatekeeping is a personal skill today—it is a basic literacy skill.

Gatekeeping as a Literacy Skill

If we decide to pay attention and adapt, then we, as educators, must first accept the responsibility of becoming our own filters of the content and other information resources that we use as teachers. In our efforts to help our students to become responsible, as a basic literacy skill, we must model and demonstrate these skills at every opportunity. Begin the first day of your class with an introduction to the author of your textbook. Describe the background, education, associations, other writings, reviews, and other information. Practice and model the importance of information about the information, of evidence that the information you are using is appropriate to the task, that we are exposing what is true.

The political response to this flood of unguarded content, and specifically to a largely manufactured (Mills) fear about Internet dangers, has been to require schools to install technology-based systems to filter out information that may be objectionable or harmful to students. Although this solution makes a great deal of sense on the surface, filtering software does not solve the problem and even exacerbates the situation in important ways.

First of all, filters are not 100 percent successful. The Henry J. Kaiser Family Foundation conducted and published a study in 2002 called *See No Evil: How Internet Filters Affect the Search for Online Health Information* (Richardson) in which they analyzed the success of six filtering products that are used widely by schools and libraries. Using three standard settings for filtering (least restrictive, intermediate, and most restrictive), they found that only 1.4 percent of all sites associated with health issues were blocked under the least restrictive setting. However, at the most restrictive setting, 24 percent of the health sites were blocked. When looking at sites on controversial issues related to health, such as "safe sex," the study found that a full 9 percent of the sites were blocked at the least restrictive setting, and 50 percent were blocked at the most restrictive setting.

To further confuse the issues, when testing how well the filtering products block pornographic sites, only about 90 percent of the sites were blocked, regardless of the setting (87 percent at least restrictive, 90 percent at intermediate settings, and 91 percent at most restrictive). It is clear that filtering software alone does not solve the problem. But, our response has been to settle back into our assumptions of safety, as we struggle to prepare our students for their reading and math tests.

Although these filtering products serve a purpose, the real danger is that we feel that the problem is solved, that we can go on schooling the same way that we always have. The mistake is believing that this is an infrastructure issue, rather than a basic literacy issue.

As an example, a student researching the use of nanotechnology in medicine might search for *bacteria attacking nanotech robots* in Google. At this writing, the Web site that surfaces to the top is NanoDocs at RYT Hospital—Dwayne Medical Center, with the caption:

. . . can monitor their health in real-time via nanotech robots, or NanoDocs, . . . genetic therapies via specific gene vectors, attacking bacteria and viruses, . . .

A major hit for the student. Clicking to the site reveals a professional-looking Web site with high resolution pictures and even several flash animations illustrating the use of nanobots for real-time health monitoring. Unfortunately, students who are accustomed to working in filtered classrooms, with government vetted textbooks, watching authoritative lecturers, using strict librarian selected reference books and periodicals, will most likely assume that the information available in this Web site is appropriate for their report, multimedia presentation, or research for an ailing relative. This student has been taught to assume the authority of the information that he or she has encounters.

On the other hand, a student who has been taught by teachers and librarians who model the critical evaluation of all content, including their textbooks, might treat this site differently. We must teach our students to ask questions about the answers that they find, and the best way to teach this is to practice it as a habit. Those questions might include:

Have you ever heard of this?

If you haven't heard of the topic, then maybe someone else has. It may surprise you that one of the best ways to ask this question is to go to Wikipedia. Part of its value is in its social basis, where people, as they learn of new topics, report them as articles, and it is often reported almost immediately. So for established and emerging topics, Wikipedia is a good place to go.

Web Resources

http://wikipedia.org/
http://news.google.com/

In addition, a Google News search will reveal if the topic has been reported recently in any of hundreds of news sources around the world.

Our NanoDocs failed both of these searches, returning no links.

Does this make sense?

Does a quick scan of the text of the site ring true? Does it sound authoritative with an interest in serving its readers? Is there any indication that the writer is trying to overtly influence you? Is there any indication of *tongue in cheek*?

Our site on NanoDocs seems to be a serious delivery of information, intended to serve, and genuinely interested in generating customers. This is especially true considering the effort involved in producing the flash animations. So our page passes this test.

Who is the source?

Looking for information on the source can be as simple as it was to find the information in question. Simply conduct a search for the source, in this case, *RYT Hospital, Dwayne Medical Center*. At this writing, I received just more than 12,000 hits—respectable. I can scan through some of the Web pages that mention the source, and look for context. For instance, the fourth Web site is the Museum of Hoaxes. That raises a flag!

I can also conduct a search for a legitimate hospital, such as *Wake Memorial Hospital*. Here I get more than 355,000 hits. Those 12,000 hits suddenly seem less respectable.

Another way to check the source is to enter the following line into a Google search.

link:http://rythospital.com

This search will reveal Web sites that link to RYH Hospital Web site, many of which are about the importance of evaluating Net content, and one site about male pregnancy. Red Flag!

Does the domain seem legitimate?

The domain is the first part of a Web site's URL. The URL of this book's Web site is:

http://davidwarlick.com/redefining_literacy/

The domain is:

http://davidwarlick.com

It is fairly easy to obtain an official looking Web domain. *davidwarlick.com* costs about $10 a year. Still, misleading Web sites will sometimes include a domain name that is unrelated to the content and the source. For instance, if the Web page for NanoDocs, generated by RYT Hospital, has a URL of:

http://davidwarlick.com/nanodocs

then it is probably at least a hoax. Also, if the URL includes an IP address, a unique number that identifies the server to the Internet, then the site is almost certainly not supported by an established organization. Such a URL might look like this one from a site that publishes facts about HIV:

http://147.129.226.1/library/research/AIDSFACTS.htm

Our NanoDocs page passes this test as well.

Who owns the domain?

This can be one of the most revealing tests you can conduct. Simply make a note of the domain of the site and point your browser to one of several Web services that facilitate domain lookups, showing who owns the domain. Entering our domain into Register.com's Whois lookup reveals that the owner of the domain is Elizabeth Preatner with an e-mail address of:

cmstransferemail@affinity.com

Searching for Elizabeth reveals one occurrence, the RYT Hospital Web site. Her e-mail address, however, does expose some truth. If we take the address and strip out the domain, affinity.com, and paste that into the browser, we learn more about the organization or service. Affinity is a Web hosting, advertising, and e-commerce service. We have to ask why a representative of RYT Hospital would be using the domain of a Web hosting company in her e-mail address. Red Flag!

What else does the site offer?

> **Knowing these rules of content and using them to seek and collect evidence of information's appropriateness is a basic literacy skill.**

Web pages are usually hierarchical in nature, with a front page to the Web site, with child pages that link from the main page. Child pages also can be parent pages to other sub-children, or subtopics. Often, we can learn more about one page by looking at its parent page. An easy way to do this is called URL backtracking.

The URL for the NanoDocs page is:

http://rythospital.com/nanodocs/

If we place the cursor at the end of this URL and delete back until we reach the next forward slash (/), and press the **Enter** key, the parent page of the current page should be revealed. In this case, it is the home page of the RYT Hospital, Dwayne Medical Center, home not only to NanoDocs, but also to Genochoice, a service that enables would-be parents to have genetic designer children, and reports on the first male pregnancy. *Does this ring true?* It's more evidence that this is a very cleverly created bogus Web site.

Each of these techniques is a critical part of exposing the source and validity of the information being considered—and they are techniques of literacy. They come less from a list of rules and established criteria for evaluating content, and much more about a knowledge of the emerging rules of media, where it comes from, how it flows, and its basic structures. Understanding these rules of

Web Resource

http://martinlutherking.org/
http://register.com/whois.rcmx

content and using them to seek and collect evidence of information's appropriateness is a part of basic literacy. It's as critical as reading.

One of my favorite scenarios finds a middle school child researching the Civil Rights movement, specifically Martin Luther King, Jr. Conducting his research at home, and away from the protection of the school's filtering software, he finds the Web site, **Martin Luther King, Jr.: A True Historical Examination**. He sees and begins to read a polished, well organized, and professional looking Web document. However, if this student has been taught to evaluate information, which means being willing to ask questions about the answers he finds, then our literate student becomes immediately suspicious of this document. That there is no mention of the documents' author or publishing organization is one clue. It is not a condition that should automatically disqualify the document from use, but it is a reason to become suspicious and to investigate further. Using information in the digital world requires us to be detectives, and it can be fun.

Our student, understanding something about how the Web works, does find the text *Contact the Web Master: Click Here. "Click Here"* is a hyperlink to the author's e-mail address. Our student researcher knows that if he clicks the link, his e-mail program will launch, addressing a new message to the Web master of the page. But if he right-clicks the link, a popup menu appears, and he selects from the pop-up menu, *Copy Link Location*. The author's e-mail address is copied into the computer's clipboard where the student can paste the address into a blank text document (SimpleText, NotePad, or TextEdit) and examine the e-mail URL.

mailto:vincent.breeding@stormfront.org

We can tell that it is an e-mail URL because the prefix is *mailto:* rather than the Web URL prefix of *http://*. We discover that the owner of the address is Vincent Breeding, and the domain of the organization that is providing him with e-mail access is *stormfront.org*.

We now have some clues about the origins of this Web page. For instance, we can enter the owner's name into a search engine and learn more about what he has written and what other people have written about him. A search in Google reveals more than 800 hits. Also, using his text processor, our student can remove the *mailto:* prefix from the e-mail URL and replace it with the Web prefix, *http://*. Then he replaces the user's e-mail name and the *at* (@) symbol with *www(dot)*. The result is a Web URL.

http://stormfront.org

Our digital investigator then copies the Web URL into his computer's clipboard and pastes it into the address bar of his browser. The

> **"** Literacy must be redefined and expanded to address a new information world that is larger in scope and smaller in access. **"**

page that loads tells all. It is a white supremacist organization.

If our student/citizen is literate only in the traditional sense, and in the sense on which students are being tested today and called successful learners, can we call them literate in today's information landscape?—or are they dangerous?

Literacy must be redefined and expanded to address a new information world that is larger in scope and yet smaller in access. We would be better off not teaching children to read, if we are not helping them to critically evaluate what they are reading. Students must learn to be suspicious of information, to ask questions, and to be ready to defend the information that they use and build with.

Investigative Strategy—More Questions

Selecting information from the global Internet requires an investigative technique as much like that of a newspaper reporter as a detective. As mentioned earlier, literacy in the 21st century includes a willingness to ask questions about the answers you find. In writing a news article, reporters try to answer five questions, or the five Ws: **Who**, **What**, **When**, **Where**, and **Why**. These Ws make a very effective basis for evaluating information available to us on the Internet for the same reasons that they have served reporters. They tend to tell the whole story.

Literacy Invoking Assignment

But before we discuss these five questions, it is important to create a context for these questions that is useful to student learning. It relates to the nature of the assignments we give our students. If the assignment is to write a report about South Africa, then almost anything goes. There is no compelling reason for the student to seriously evaluate the information he or she finds beyond determining that it is about South Africa and that it is true. A newspaper editor would not ask a reporter to write a piece about South Africa unless there was a *story* in it and unless that story impacts on people in some way.

Teachers might think of themselves as the editor-in-chief of their classroom, asking students to produce pieces that result in a story that will affect people in some way. If the students are asked to write a report that supports the continued financial support for that nation or discontinuance of funding, then the students' work has a goal. Not only is this a more authentic assignment, but it also gives the students a realistic basis for evaluating the information that they find that supports the report. Students ask the question, "How does this information help me accomplish my goal?"

Who?

When addressing the **who** part of our evaluation of an information source, we are seeking information about the author, publisher, or actor within the context of our goal. "What is it about the author or the publishing organization that helps me support continued financial aid?" Deep within this question is an implied question, "Is this information the truth?" We will discuss truth later, but for now, is it evident (is there evidence) that the author or publishing organization has expertise in the area or has had experiences that gives them valid and relevant knowledge in the subject being considered?

If you have the name, or even the e-mail address of the author, there is much you can do to investigate the source of your information. Use the same Internet search engine that connected you with the information in order to investigate the author. When you enter the author's name (inside quotes) or even the e-mail address into a large search engine, you should learn more about the author, access other documents he or she has published, and learn what other people have to say about the person—each adding to your body of evidence.

What?

Another question to ask is "**What**?" What is the content you have found? What does it mean? How does it agree or disagree with other sources of information on the same topic? Some sub-questions to ask that might help you to determine any bias or hidden agenda include:

- Does the information affect you on an emotional level?

- Does the information promote anger or ill-will toward other people or their ideas?

- Does the information make significant use of multimedia in communicating an idea?

- Does the information in any way threaten you or make you feel ill at ease?

An affirmative to any of these sub-questions should raise a flag of suspicion. It does not mean that the information should be discarded, but it does indicate that someone is trying to convince you of an idea that may be difficult to sell without a clear and logical consideration of facts. Continue to investigate.

In terms of the assignment, does the nature of the information help you accomplish your goal? How does the information look? Does its format (prose, data, image, animation, video) help you accomplish your goal?

When?

"**When**" can be a tricky question. It is a critical question, but we should not automatically assume that the more recent document is necessarily the better one. It depends on what the researcher is trying to achieve. If the student is investigating America's move toward war in 1941, documents dated at that time may be the most valuable and critical to the assignment, under most circumstances. The evidence the student seeks is, "How does the publishing or revision date of the document help accomplish the goal of the assignment?" "In what way does it contribute to the story or the position?"

It can be difficult to determine the date of an online document if the author has not posted it as part of the page. However, one way to determine date is to use **The Way Back Machine**. This service has been archiving Web pages since 1996 and currently holds historic versions of more than 85 billion Web pages. It employs Web crawlers (small programs that methodically move around on the Web) that periodically take photographs, so to speak, of Web pages and archives those pages in its library. It allows us to see what those pages looked like and what they said over the months and years. For instance, I am considering Web pages about the nation of Syria and have found a site called SyriaGate. The page does not post any dates for its initial publishing or subsequent revisions. So I go to **The Way Back Machine** and enter the travel site's URL,

http://syriagate.com.

Upon clicking the submit button, I receive a list of dates on which that particular page was archived. The most recent, as of the writing of this book, was on August 24, 2007, about six months ago. I can click that date to see what the page said then and compare with the content one year later. There are more than 350 other dates going back to November 28, 1999. So even when I cannot establish the current date of a document, I can find reference points. If you are using FireFox as your browser, you can select **Page Info** from the **Tools** menu and learn more about the page, often including the date that the file was created and last modified.

Where?

When writing a newspaper article, the reporter considers geography when answering the "**Where**" question. Even though geography may be a factor critical to the goal of the assignment, the student should also consider where the author or publishing organization sits within a political or ideological spectrum. Is there anything about the information or the author that would lead you to believe that their information is less than true, in terms of accom-

Web Resource

http://archive.org/web/web.php

plishing your goals, or are they attempting to manipulate the truth in some way to accomplish an agenda? Related to **"where"** is **"why."** What does the author have to gain by publishing this information? Is there any evidence that the author would gain from reporting something less than the truth?

In the scenario with the Martin Luther King, Jr. site, we learned by investigating the organization that provided the author with an e-mail address that chances were high that he was influenced by ideologies that were dramatically to the right on the political spectrum.

The Digital Index Card (See Figure 2.14: Digital Index Card) is an online tool that can help student researchers to evaluate information they are considering by asking these questions. It provides a Web form for the student's name, project title and description, the student's e-mail address, and the evaluation questions. After completing, the tool will generate a Web document that can help the student decide if the information is appropriate. An e-mail is also sent to the student's address with the same content. There is also a printable version of this file available at the book's resource Web site.

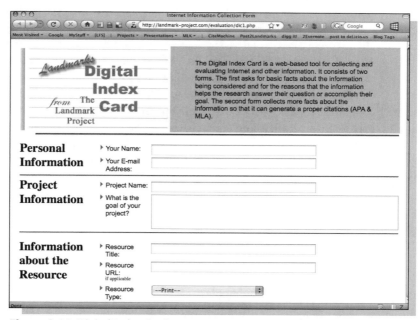

Figure 2.14: Digital Index Card

Web Resource

http://landmark-project.com/evaltool/

Investigative Strategy—Defend Your Information

The detective metaphor should be carried a little bit further. Our students have sought their information, acting like detectives, searching for clues and evidence about the information that helps them accomplish their goals, refining their search strategies, and uncovering information solutions. They have investigated their findings, looking for accuracy, bias, and validity. They must now be prepared to defend their information.

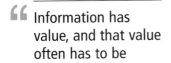
> **Information has value, and that value often has to be demonstrated.**

In the information age information has value. But that value must often be demonstrated. As our information environment continues to shift toward a more open arena, an idea exchange, practitioners need to be able to provide evidence that information is true, without value-depleting bias, and appropriate to the task at hand.

Ask students to defend their information. Hold court, so to speak. Ask classmates to jury the efforts to establish the information's value. You might actually ask your class, as an assignment, to answer a question by researching the Internet. The more controversial the issue is, the better the assignment, though you must be careful about the degree of controversy you want to introduce to your class. One example might be, "Should the United States continue its manned space exploration programs?" Inform the students that they will not be graded on their answer, but on how well they can defend the information they use to support their answer. Part of the assignment is to be able to provide evidence that the information they found is:

- True
- Consistent with other sources
- Authoritative
- Dependable
- Reliable
- Without value-depleting bias
- Applicable to the question being addressed

You can carry this activity all the way to a mock courtroom with judge, jury, prosecuting and defending attorneys, and courtroom reporters. Or you can simply institute a practice of questioning sources in your classroom.

It is only fair and appropriate that your students be invited to question the information that they are being taught from. They should be encouraged to challenge the textbook, reference books from the library, Web resources, and the news. When we are asked to backup the information we use, and can do so successfully, then we are doing simply what we should be doing—teaching in the 21st century. We're practicing contemporary literacy.

Conclusion

Exposing what is true is the longest and most involved section of this book. Although each of the contemporary literacies covered equips us as lifelong learners, exposing what is true is probably the most useful as a learning literacy. If you attend educational technology conferences, you hear a lot about online courses. Providing instruction over the networks solves many problems related to educating a dispersed nation and world. However, a majority of the distance learning that people will be engaged in will be of a more casual nature. It will simply mean using your information landscape (electronic or otherwise) to learn what you need to know, in order to do what you need to do, right now!

Being literate in the 21st century means that we are beginning to think beyond the place we can see and the moment we experience. It means that we increasingly identify ourselves by what we know, and that what we know springs from a vast, dynamic, growing, global, increasingly accessible, and powerfully searchable world of information—and from people with whom we can share that information.

> " Distance learning … will simply mean using the Network (electronic or otherwise) to learn what you need to know, in order to do what you need to do – right now! "

To take advantage of this digital realm, we must be plugged in, both literally and figuratively. We must have access to the devices through which digital information is provided, and the knowledge and skills to use those devices in order to interact with that world happily and productively.

Action Items

Directors of Technology

- Create a standard page with the district's banner that includes links to appropriate search tools and other Web-based information searching resources so that the page becomes, among other things, a doorway to the global Internet. This page can then be linked to by school, media center, and special project sites in the district. Continue to maintain the site adding new search tools and techniques as they become available.

- The AUPs that we instituted five years ago addressed the needs of a read-only Web. Review your current district Acceptable Use Policy to assure that it addresses a read/write Web environment, where teachers and students are able and encouraged not only to access information from the Internet, but also to participate in and publish to the Web.

- Look at regular communications that go out from the district's central office, and identify those that might become more valuable if they are also syndicated with RSS feeds.

- Establish policies regarding access to inappropriate information at school that emphasize proactive guidance, appropriate instructional practices, observation and evaluation of student use, and address filtering and blocking technologies required by the U.S. government.

- Configure all systems so that each teacher (and student if possible) can establish personal information digital libraries that follow the person from station to station, perhaps a Web-based service. Consider utilizing an open source online bookmarking services, such as Scuttle.

- Work with other curriculum leaders to integrate proper research and self-teaching into classroom activities consistent with 21st century technologies, culture, and literacy.

- Investigate opportunities to establish after-hours access to computers and the Internet for students and families who do not have convenient access. Work with local service organizations to renovate an empty store downtown and establish a community cybercafé.

Principals and Head Teachers

- Integrate into your teacher evaluation system the expectation that teachers will integrate digital information materials into their lessons on a daily basis and to discuss with their students the literacy skills they use to find, identify, and evaluate the information.

- Work toward improving each classroom's capacity to make digital networked content a part of every lesson.

- To the greatest degree possible, expect students to turn in their assignments digitally by e-mail, on disk, Web drop box, or other method. They should be working with digital content and producing digital work.

- Work toward improving each student's capacity to work with digital content on a daily basis.

Web Resource

http://sourceforge.net/projects/scuttle/

- Arrange computer and Internet facilities in your school in a way that offers the most access to the most people possible, and in a way that affords flexibility in their use. Learning to use technology is not a high priority. Learning to learn with technology is.

- Arrange supervised after-hours access to computers for students and families who do not have convenient access at home. Establish a school cybercafé.

Media Specialists

- Collect and maintain a list of local residents with expertise who will make themselves available to classrooms for either face-to-face interaction with students or via Internet communication (e-mail, chat, message board, or video conference).

- Investigate opportunities to connect with experts over the Internet who might contribute to specific units taught by your teachers.

- Maintain a Web site that offers links to Internet resources related to topics being studied in your teachers' classrooms. Treat these pages as reserve lists.

- Establish and use a personal digital information library. If it is not useful, then reorganize it and try again. Help teachers in establishing their own personal digital information libraries and integrate them with yours.

- Regularly evaluate Weblogs related to the topics that teachers are teaching, and recommend appropriate bloggers for them to read.

- Create inviting and comfortable stations for students to conduct research in known as *knowledge gardens*. Go browse around Barnes and Noble for ideas and cybercafés for ideas.

School Tech Facilitators

- Map the school's curriculum in a way that you and the media specialist have access to what is currently being taught by each teacher, and provide services accordingly.

- Facilitate an ongoing but casual professional development environment that encourages teachers to discuss, share, and ask about digital teaching (and learning) resources available on the Net and elsewhere.

- Attend all department or grade level meetings, and be ready to suggest strategies and resources as needed.

- Aggregate news searches for the topics currently being taught in your school, and syndicate them to teachers appropriately.

- Establish a mailing list or other group messaging system, and announce new resources and research tools to the teachers and other instructional staff. As much as possible, be able to forward such messages to specific categories (social studies teachers, for example) of educators.

Teachers

- Maintain a list of your students' parents with areas of expertise, hobbies, and travels. Make sure that you have e-mail addresses for these parents for convenient communication.

- Establish and use a personal digital information library. If it is not useful, then reorganize it and try again.

- As much as possible, bring Internet-based content into the classrooms. As you present the information, describe how you found it and defend the information. Describe the questions you asked while evaluating the information and the basis for answering the questions.

- Make digital networked content a part of every assignment or lesson. Be able to identify the technology you need to increase your capacity to include digital networked content in your classroom, and share that with your local purchase agent.

- With each lesson that you teach, do a quick search of a news search tool to add something that is current.

Students

- With each research assignment that you receive, do a significant amount of the research over the Internet. If your teacher will not accept Internet research, ask why, and wait for a good answer that relates to your future.

- Search not only for information in the form of text, but also images, animations, sound, and video.

- Turn in as many of your assignments as you can in digital format (disk, CD-ROM, over the Internet). If your teacher will not accept them, ask why, and wait for a good answer that relates to your future.

- Create multimedia. Turn in as many of your assignments as you can with text, images, sound, and video. If your teacher will not accept them, ask why, and wait for a good answer that relates to your future.

Parents

- Make sure that each of your children has access to a computer connected to the Internet. This does not mean that each child should have his own computer, but that they each have access.

- When they are conducting research, sit and watch. If you have experience, help. Ask them to explain what they are finding and how it applies to what they are learning in class.

- If your children's teachers are not accepting assignments turned in digitally or limit the use of the Internet and other digital resources in their assignments, ask why, and wait for a good answer.

- When teachers do engage in activities that make creative and exciting use of digital information, share it with other parents and community members. Send an e-mail to the teacher commending her for her vision, and copy it to the principal, media specialist, and school tech facilitator.

CHAPTER 3

Employing the Information

F or some of us, our early years took place in the middle of the 20th century. Upon leaving school, many of our classmates took employment in mills and factories in larger and small towns. It had been that way for decades, and we had no reason to expect things to change. The raw materials that they worked with were fibers, magnesium, steel, plastic, and tin. Their jobs were to fashion these raw materials into products that had value.

> " In the Information Age, information is the Raw Material with which people will work. "

At the beginning of the 21st century, many of these manufacturing jobs are moving to other parts of the world and the work will increasingly be accomplished by robotics. Machines are fast, tireless, cheap, and expendable. The information that drives these machines will be written, refined, managed, and communicated by people. The products will continued to be made from mined, processed, and, increasingly, engineered materials. But the making will be done with information. In the Information Age, information is the Raw Material with which people will work.

Capacity for Information

Many of us remember growing up with one television that the entire family shared, and it was able to tune into three networks, and, if we were lucky, an independent station. We had a choice of four video media sources, and what we watched at a certain time was determined by their programming. If you wanted to watch a program, you had to be at the TV when the station or network aired that program.

Today, there are four televisions in our houses, each connected to a cable service that provides access to hundreds of channels of video content (and even more of audio content). Through that same cable line, we connect to the Internet with unimaginable access to text, audio, video, and animation on-demand at our personal computers. For a significant portion of each day, we all spend time at our computers consuming. The products that we are consuming are not made of magnesium, steel, or plastic. They are information products—an assembly of information raw materials.

We are establishing an amazing technical capacity for information. During the writing of the first edition of this book, Paul Gilster, a columnist and author of the book *Digital Literacy*, reported in a column, that ". . . hard disks will continue to grow in capacity, with 300 gigabyte drives common by year's end (2003)." At this writing, Hitachi sells a hard drive that can be installed inside of your computer that will store one terabyte (1,000 gigabytes) of information. In April 2007, Darren Murph reported in the blog, Engadget, that a new record had just been set, that Internet2 technicians sent over nine gigabytes of information 20,000 miles in one second. That is approximately 80 times the speed record set just before the first edition of this book was published.

These astounding increases in capacity beg the questions, "Where will all of this content come from?" or "Will the concept of reruns take on a whole new meaning?" In the future there will be an enormous demand for information products, and many, if not most, of today's students will be involved in producing this content. They will grow up to be information construction workers, processing, manipulating, and assembling information raw materials into unique and valuable information experiences. They will utilize a wide variety of new digital tools to work the information raw materials, molding them into new content and new meaning that people will value. Many of them are already developing and practicing the skills.

Web Resources

Centauri Dreams - http://centauri-dreams.org/
Engadget – http://engadget.com/

Product to Process

If this idea of information-based work is a reasonable speculation of the future of many of our children's lives and work, then we need to rethink our models of education—what and how we teach. Traditionally, we have considered information to be the end product of an education, that if the student knew a prescribed body of information, then he or she was educated. In a rapidly changing world, where the answers to questions are going to be changing, then what our children know will be less important than what they know how to do with it. Rather than being the end product for students to simply memorize, information should become a raw material that students learn to do something with.

This is not a brand new idea. What is new, however, is that information today is so much more workable (digital) and so many more people will be working with information in the future, and this shift must be reflected in what and how we teach. It is actually not a difficult task to imagine. There are already many people who are working the information. If we want our students to develop and practice these skills, then we should simply think of who and under what conditions someone would need to use the information that we are teaching, and then simulate such an activity for students. In those few instances that there is no person or profession that would use the information, then perhaps we should reconsider teaching it.

Employing Text

Text was the preeminent form of our information products in the 20th century, and it will continue to play an important part in how we communicate knowledge and ideas. For one thing, there is a lot of it out there, and a significant number of people can decode it for meaning. In addition, it takes a fairly low level of technology to share information in text. It can even be printed on paper.

Issues of Intellectual Property

Another useful aspect of text is that it can be indexed, making it easy to mine the information using tools such as Google or Technorati. Only a couple of decades ago, when asked to write a report, we were limited to two or three sets of encyclopedias and the reference books that were available in our local library. That information was valuable. It was produced, published in print, distributed, and organized by professionals. It cost us the time and effort to find the information and rewrite it, paraphrasing as much as we could, because using someone else's information in her words was frowned upon.

It is relevant to note that in most Asian countries, it is considered an expression of respect to copy someone else's ideas, a concept many of us would readily have seized upon, as we worked to paraphrase intelligent and polished pieces of information into our sometimes clumsy way of explaining things. Of course, we were being taught to write, not copy, so we understood. In the experience of my early education, ethics were not the issue.

The ethical use of information will be covered extensively in a later chapter. It is essential to state here and at all opportunities, that information is property, and that the intellectual property of other people should be respected. Students and teachers must learn and practice the art of crediting the ideas of others, as we will expect our ideas to be credited. It is difficult to predict how new information processing tools and immediate access to a global library of digital content will affect writing. But it is fair to say that many of these effects will be determined by the people who are currently in our classrooms.

Indexed Content

There are many ways that digital text can be employed for teaching and for learning. For instance, one of the unique qualities of networked digital text is that it can be indexed. This gives us some new opportunities for working that information to accomplish goals. As an example, if a science teacher is preparing a unit on weather, she might go to Google News and search the word *hurricane*. At this writing, more than 56,000 stories, from news services around the world, are returned—all published in the past week. The top five stories were published 17, 19, 22, 24, and 34 minutes ago.

The search produces an RSS feed that can be subscribed to by the teacher, thus producing an information product that is dynamically updating the teachers with the latest news related to this example of extreme weather. The feed can even be published through Wiki pages.

As another example, we can ask students to teach themselves about U.S. history by giving them a text file that includes all of the inaugural addresses of the presidents of the United States. Such a file can be accessed from Landmarks for Schools. The students are then asked to open the file into their word processor. Students can then employ this information by searching for keywords related to their studies, easily finding each time that a president uttered those words. Students can isolate those instances and then conduct further research to draw conclusions about the history of the United States.

Web Resources

YouTube - http://youtube.com/
Technorati - http://technorati.com/
Presidential Inaugural Addresses -
      http://landmark-project.com/Inaugural_Addresses.html

As the Web becomes more sophisticated, it starts to serve as a platform for such activities. Yale Law School's Avalon Project has archived primary source documents, categorized by pre-18th century, 18th century, 19th, 20th, and 21st centuries. The site features a search tool enabling researchers to query the entire collection, a unique cross-section of U.S. history, for keywords and phrases. For instance, a search of *defense* returned context-rich utterances by: Harrison, Harding, Monroe, Adams, Truman, Taft, Buchanan, Eisenhower, Coolidge, Reagan, Jackson, Adams, Clinton, Cleveland, F. Roosevelt, and Pierce.

The Web has become more sophisticated over the past several years. Many describe the new Web as becoming much more than just a source for information and a place to collaborate. It is an emerging platform for working content. The practice of indexing content has extended beyond Web pages. One example is BlogPulse, which is indexing nearly 80 million blogs at this writing (July 2008), and capturing more than 90 million blog posts in a typical 24-hour period.

This innovative search tool works its information in a uniquely powerful way. As an example, we might search for blog posts that mention *"heart disease."* The search engine returns approximately 30,000 articles. Near the top of the report page is a clickable icon labeled, *Trend This.* When we click this link, BlogPulse generates a line graph that illustrates the number of blog entries mentioning our search term over the past six months (See Figure 3.1: BlogPulse1).

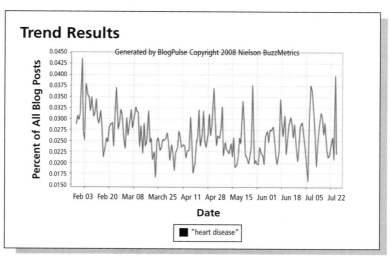

Figure 3.1: BlogPulse 1

Web Resources

Avalon Project - http://yale.edu/lawweb/avalon/avalon.htm
BlogPulse - http://blogpulse.com/

This sort of ready analysis of the blogosphere (an ongoing human conversation on just about everything) is unique. In a 2004 blog post, Dave Sifry, the CEO of Technorati, another blog search engine, said that the blogosphere is the "exhaust of our attention streams . . ." (Sifry, Oct 2004). We are laying down our daily observations, reflections, and conversations, and with an increasingly rich and powerful Web, we are able to mine that content and express it efficiently.

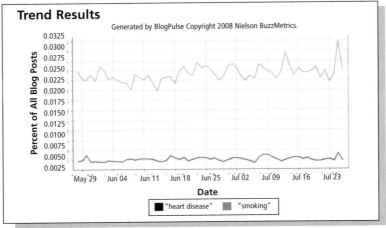

Figure 3.2: BlogPulse 2

BlogPulse enables us to re-trend our search term, factoring in other terms such as smoking, producing the two-month plotting in Figure 3.2.

The new Web also has given us some new ways of working text content to help it tell its story. Tag clouds are one such technique for visualizing text-based content. Tag clouds list the most used words in a body of text, such as a collection of blog entries. They further illustrate the value of these individual words by sizing them based on the number of occurrences. The tag cloud in Figure 3.3 represents the most recent 30 blog entries in the author's blog, 2¢

Blog Entries

across among answers anyway arts believe blog care children color come conference content conversation conversations create creative credit days decoration edubloggercon education educators elearning event finally folks font future game games google halverson having help hope hours index information kevin learn learning life listening live making minutes morning music myself necc networks njelite none notes open padding people photos play playing plurk position post presentation question questions rather real relative said session sessions skills social society source span start statistics story students suspect tagcloud tags talk teachers teaching technology technorati text thanks three told twitter video warlick ways wikipedia work working world year

Figure 3.3: Tag Cloud

Web Resource

Technorati - http://technorati.com/

Worth. The words, which are displayed alphabetically, show more common words in larger fonts and less often used words in the smaller fonts. As a result, you get a visual, at-a-glance peek at what this blog is about. It is about *education*, *students*, and *teachers*. I also talk about *information* and *learning*.

On April 27, 2007, Pollster, a political blog, posted an entry that included tag clouds representing the transcripts from the Democratic presidential debates. On May 4, they posted the report for the Republican candidates. Studying these content maps reveals clues about the candidates and what they like to talk about.

Another interesting example is Flickr. This online photo archive tool will be discussed more in the next section. At this point, it is important to note that Flickr is an online photo album where photographers, amateur and professional, can upload their digital images for friends, family, neighbors, and the world to view and even comment about. As photographers upload their photos, they can tag them with words that label the images. A photo of uncle John at cousin Janet's wedding might be tagged with *family*, *wedding*, *tipsy*, and *Poconos*. The Flickr Web site includes a tag cloud that illustrates the most used tags in its photos. They also include smaller tag clouds for tags used in the last week and in the last 24 hours.

It has been an interesting progression to watch as its tag cloud evolved Flickr's usership, expanding beyond the initial tech-savvy, early adopters, who took photos of their newest mobile phones and the insides of their homemade computers, tagging them appropriately, to the more mainstream community of people who tag their photos with *party*, *travel*, *vacation*, and *wedding*.

As a user tool, tag clouds are fairly easy to implement in your own information experiences. If you are a blogger, you can include a tag cloud of your blog articles by using MakeCloud. Simply go to the URL posted below and paste into the text box the URL of your blog's RSS feed. Pressing the **Make Cloud** button will generate a sample display of your blog's tag cloud. It will also give you a single line of code that, when pasted into the sidebar of your blog, will display your blog's tag cloud.

Web Resources

Pollster - http://pollster.com/
Democratic Debates - http://pollster.com/blogs/tag_clouds_for_the_democratic.php
Republican Debates - www.pollster.com/blogs/tag_clouds_for_the_republican.php
Flickr - http://flickr.com/
Flickr Tag Cloud - http://flickr.com/photos/tags/
MakeCloud - http://makecloud.com/

Figure 3.4: DIY Tag Cloud

Another interesting and flexible tool is TagCrowd. This tool provides a scrolling text box, into which you can paste the text you would like to cloud. For instance, pasting the Declaration of Independence into the text box and clicking the **Visualize** button generates the following tag cloud (See Figure 3.4: DIY Tag Cloud).

Working Tabular Data

A more striking way that digital information can be employed is the use of tabular data. The Internet holds an enormous amount of data that are published by universities, research centers, and the government covering an astounding range of topics. Data can be found that describe the weather, air quality, sports, labor, geography, demographics, crime, biology, economics, and many other subjects. One of my favorites is the Advanced National Seismic System (ANSS). Their Web site provides an online catalog (database) of seismic events, a composite of several other catalogs maintained by various agencies and organizations. The ANSS database is searchable so that you can identify the types of earthquakes you want to learn about, and it will generate a data set on those quakes. For example, when you go to the **ANSS Catalog Search** page and indicate, using a Web form, that you are interested in seismic events beginning *2004/12/01,00:00:00* and ending *2005/01/01,00:00:00* (Quakes during the month of December 2004) indicating at least *3.0* in magnitude on the Richter scale, it generates 51 pages of data on individual quakes from around the world. The data includes the date and time of each event, its latitude and longitude, the magnitude, depth at the epicenter, and additional information that I do not even understand.

> **Web Resources**
>
> Add TagCrowd - http://tagcrowd.com/
> ANSS Catalog Search - http://ncedc.org/anss/catalog-search.html

Using the mouse, you can highlight the entire data set, copy it into the computer's clipboard, and then paste the data directly into an empty Microsoft Excel spreadsheet. Unfortunately, the entire table of data flows into only the first column of the spreadsheet. But we can spread the data out and format by doing the following:

1. Highlight the first column.

2. Pull down the **Data** menu and selecting **Text to Columns**.

3. A series of wizards appear, each asking how the information is to be formatted. In the first wizard, determine how the columns should be identified or delimitated. If, in the preview box toward the bottom of the window, the columns seem to line up, then select **Fixed Width**. If they do not, then select **Delimited**. Delimited means that there is a character, usually a tab or a comma, between the items that separate the columns.

4. If you selected Fixed Width, then use the next wizard window to move the column breaks around and even add new ones, or delete existing ones.

5. In the next wizard window, select each column and determine how the information should be formatted. Selecting **General** will treat the information in this column as a value that can be calculated in a formula. This is for columns that are exclusively numbers. Columns that hold text would be marked as **Text**. If the column contains a date or time, then selecting **Date** will have the information formatted in the date/time layout of your choosing. Finally, if there is a column that is not necessary for your purposes, then click the **Do not import column (Skip)** radio button.

6. When the **Finish** button is clicked, the pasted information is converted into a spreadsheet.

In our example of the earthquake data, you import only the *date, longitude*, and *latitude* of each seismic event. In case you are following along with your own experiment, it is important that the latitude data be to the right of the longitude data. To accomplish this, highlight the latitude column and cut it. Then highlight the column to the right of the longitude and paste. To cause this data to actually tell you something, highlight the block of data, the longitude and latitude, and click the graphing tool icon.

There is much that you can do to label and format a graph. I simply select the **Scatter Plot** graph and then click finish. The resulting graph marks X/Y coordinates to the longitude/latitude values of the earthquakes (See Figure 3.5: Earthquake Map). The horizontal zero (0) line represents the Equator, while the vertical zero (0) line represents the Prime Meridian. The dots generated by the plot represent individual seismic events of at least 3.0 on the Richter scale occurring during the month of December 2004. The result is a rather dramatic representation of the planet's tectonic plates, the ring of fire around the Pacific Rim, and more. Text data are helping us to see. They tell a story.

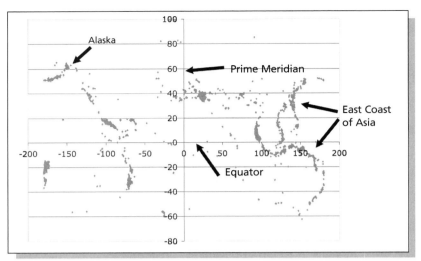

Figure 3.5: Earthquake Map

Data telling their story is at the heart of IBM's Many Eyes. The project is maintained by the Visual Communication Lab, which provides data sets for visualization and also the ability to upload your own data sets. Your information can then be displayed in a number of ways, including: maps, line, stack, and bar graphs, block, bubble, and matrix charts, scatter plots, network diagrams, pie charts, tree maps, tag clouds, and word trees. Their goal is to enable communities of people who want to employ information by visualizing it in ways that add value.

Processing digital text is a practice that many of us take for granted today. It seems un-extraordinary any more. Yet, it is predicted that in 2008, we will generate more information than in all of human history before the end of 2007. When information is so abundant and drives so much of our experiences, it is essential to remember that digital information is made to be worked, and we should practice it as part of our jobs as educators.

Employing Web Content—Advanced

Let's return back to the Flickr tags to examine how its tag clouds have evolved over time, which is not a difficult task because of another information tool that is unique, important, and can come in handy for teachers. The Wayback Machine is part of the Web site, Internet Archive. The goal of this amazing and

Web Resources

Many Eyes - http://services.alphaworks.ibm.com/manyeyes/
The Visual Communication Lab - http://research.ibm.com/visual/
Flickr Tags - http://flickr.com/photos/tags/
The Wayback Machine - http://archive.org/web/web.php/
Internet Archive - http://archive.org/

much used site is to become the Library of Alexandria of the 21st century, a place where people can upload their content from videos of important speeches to home videos for free. The Wayback Machine employs Internet spiders, small programs, that crawl the Web examining Web pages and taking what are essentially photographs of the pages. The result is almost two petabytes (a quadrillion letters, symbols, and numbers) of archived Web pages, going back to early 1996.

Enter the URL for Flickr's tag cloud page, and scan through the 37 times that the page has been captured and recorded, starting on June 7, 2004. It is possible to use a bit of basic PHP programming to capture all of the tags and to score their frequency of use and then produce a Web page that can compare and plot specific tags, tracking where they appear and disappear as frequently used tag labels, producing a mashup of that data.

So, is being able to use computer programming to dynamically scrape data from a Web page and cook it up for visualization a basic literacy? At present, the answer is "No!" However, understanding that information can be mined and employed in value-adding ways is a basic literacy. And, if it helps you accomplish your goals, being able to teach yourself how to do it is a basic literacy.

Employing Images

Today, nearly every classroom has access to a digital camera. Many classrooms have their own camera that is used nearly every day. According to a February 2007 Register article, between 80 and 90 million digital cameras were sold in 2006. When we factor in that most of the 500 million mobile phones that were sold in the same year also had digital photography features, capturing the images around us has become important (Maxim).

> There are lots of reasons why people are purchasing cameras that connect to their computers, but the most important reason is that the picture taking is only the first step in the process of picture making. The fundamental difference between digital pictures and the traditional chemically processed variety is the fact that each dot in the picture (pixel) is represented by a number or a series of numbers. Computers love numbers and can alter them in an instant. When managing large quantities of related numbers, the computer can produce some fascinating results.

Mixing Visuals

Four years ago, my wife and I traveled to Scotland for a conference, spending a few days in Inverness and exploring the Highlands before the event. Since both of us have ancestors from Scotland, who fought with the Jacobites against King George II, we took the short bus ride from Inverness to the site of the Battle of Colloden.

Figure 3.6: Image Doctoring

Being a very cold September day, there was no one else on the grounds, so the two of us took turns photographing each other standing by the memorial. After returning home, we loaded both photographs into a computer. You can see them as item A and B in Figure 3.6.

Using a lasso tool, a software feature that is common among many image editing programs, we drew along the figures of my wife and myself and then cut and pasted the cutouts back into the image. You can see the results in items C and D in Figure 3.6, where our cutouts are now separate layers that can be moved around on top of the original photograph. These layers can also change positions, so that our cutouts can be made to appear beneath the larger image.

Then I copied the cutout of myself and pasted it into the photograph of my wife, so that we were both on the same page. Resizing myself to a height in more accurate relation to wife's, and then placing her image layer above my own, placing her in front of me, the image was done, and we had a photo of the two of us together at the battle ground. It's cheating, but we were both there.

Figure 3.7: Photo Before   **Figure 3.8:** Photo After

Some effects can be made much more easily such as that in Figure 3.7 and Figure 3.8. Here, you see two pictures taken in Saint Ives, England. The first is the original black and white photograph taken with a standard digital camera.

The effect of the second version of the picture was accomplished by loading the picture into an image processing program and applying a filter *cutout*. The filter is a set of programs that sifts through all of the numbers involved in defining each pixel (individual dot) in the photograph. In the case of the *cutout*, it takes pixels that are in the same general location with similar values, averages their values, and then applies the processed values back to the pixels. The effect is a picture that looks as though it were designed by an illustrator.

Many professional graphic artists use a program from Adobe called Photoshop. However, to use this powerful and highly flexible tool requires some knowledge about graphic art and a considerable amount of time to learn it. In addition, PhotoShop is prohibitively expensive for many schools. As an alternative, Adobe has released a less sophisticated version called PhotoShop Elements. It is a scaled-down version of the professional product and costs less than $100.

There are other options for image editing software. Gimp is a sophisticated open source (free software maintained by a community of volunteer programmers) graphics program that is available for free download for Linux and Windows computers. All Macintosh computers come with iPhoto, an image cataloging program that includes some editing tools. An equivalent to iPhoto for Windows computers is Picasa, a project from Google.

Web Resources

Gimp http://gimp.org/
Picasa http://picasa.google.com/

Figure 3.9: Palm 1

Figure 3.10: Palm 2

Figure 3.11: Palm 3

Figure 3.12: Palm 4

As illustrated in the photo in Scotland, one of the most useful features of Photoshop Elements, Gimp, and other more sophisticated programs is layering. Remember how we used layering to get the photos of the two tourists on the same image. Here is an application that may be more applicable for educators. With layering, you can have many different pictures stacked on top of each other, so individual components or layers can be altered independently. Look at the picture in Figure 3.9 of a Handspring Visor PDA.

For a teacher who is going to start using a set of hand-held computing devices, it would be wise to produce a document that describes to students how to use these tools. In this case, a photograph is taken with a digital camera (See Figure 3.9: Palm 1), loaded to a computer, and opened into PhotoShop Elements.

A new *layer* is created on which information can be painted, pasted, or typed without affecting the original photograph. On this layer, *On/Off Switch* is typed. (See Figure 3.10: Palm 2)

To better highlight the text, a new layer is added between the text layer and the original picture. On this layer, a white rectangle is created to go behind the text. (See Figure 3.11: Palm 3)

In the third evolution of this picture (See Figure 3.12: Palm 4) the layer with the rectangle is set to produce a shadow to better distinguish this information from the original image. A new layer is also created with a line and arrow. That layer is moved so that the beginning of the line rests behind the rectangle.

In this example, we have taken a photograph and utilized some basic graphics techniques with tools that are not only available to professional graphic designers, but increasingly to anyone who wishes to employ visual information to accomplish a goal.

A recent study conducted by the PEW Internet and American Life Project found that 64 percent of online teenagers ages 12 to 17 engage in at least one type of digital content creation—up from 57 percent in 2004. They are employing text for their blogs and social networks, images for their photo galleries, and even video (Lenhart).

Employing Audio

In 1986, Twentieth Century Fox produced and distributed a movie that spawned at least four sequels, two TV series, and one animated series. There was little about the movie *Highlander* that would indicate its future success. The story involves a race of sword-wielding immortals who travel through the centuries surviving by loping off the heads of other immortals and trying not to lose their own. Performances by European-born Christopher Lambert and an aging, stiff, but compelling Sean Connery had less to do with the success of this movie than the soundtrack and the superb editing that tied together vision and music.

The seductively dark atmosphere was in no small measure enhanced by the lush music composed and performed by John Deacon, Brian May, Roger Taylor, and Freddie Mercury, the '80s rock band, Queen. The cinematography of the Scottish Highlands and the highly synthesized music combined to create a movie experience that was difficult to see only once.

We need to be reminded from time to time that we enjoy our experience through many senses. Though most of us identify more with sight than we do with the other senses, what we hear, smell, touch, and taste are each essential in defining our reality, and communication is merely one person's attempt at sharing aspects of his reality with others.

There is a student-produced video that is often played at education technology conferences. The visual aspects, by themselves, are not especially impressive. In fact, they consist mostly of still images and text messages that float or quiver across the screen. But the background audio, the hauntingly beautiful *Sacrifice* by Lisa Gerrard and Pieter Bourke, turns the communication into a highly emotional experience. Music communicates to many of us in a way that even the most well-crafted words will not. Music can turn our emotions; and where the emotions go, the mind and body will follow.

There is a problem, though, with integrating music into student-produced information products. Receiving permission to use copyrighted information from the music (and video) industry is probably more difficult to achieve than most other sources. In fact, *impossible* is probably more accurate. Several years ago, I was delivering a conference presentation about copyright. Before the session began, I was playing Glenn Miller's *In the Mood* to wake up the post lunchtime audience. During the presentation, a teacher asked how I went

Figure 3.13: Midi Keyboard

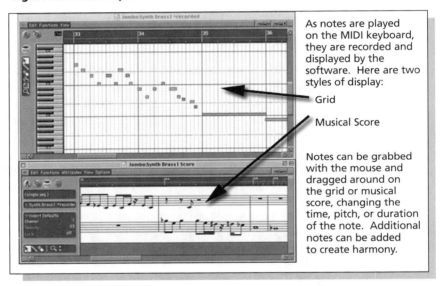

As notes are played on the MIDI keyboard, they are recorded and displayed by the software. Here are two styles of display:

Grid

Musical Score

Notes can be grabbed with the mouse and dragged around on the grid or musical score, changing the time, pitch, or duration of the note. Additional notes can be added to create harmony.

Figure 3.14: Midi Software

about getting permission to play Glenn Miller before the session began. I was stumped and stopped dead in my tracks, and I have not played anyone else's music to a paying audience since. However, this gave me an opportunity to pursue an interest I'd had for some time. I invested in a synthesizer, a musical keyboard that can synthesize or imitate a variety of existing and invented instruments. The keyboard that I purchased (See Figure 3.13: Midi Keyboard), has MIDI capabilities, as do most synthesizers. MIDI (Musical Instrument Digital Interface) means that the keyboard can exchange information with a computer. As notes are played on the keyboard, the corresponding data that describe each note (pitch, tone, instrument, duration) are sent to the computer, where software (See Figure 3.14: Midi Software) stores it for later processing. Data can also be sent from the computer to the keyboard, causing it to play the music that is stored and encoded by the computer into a digital message.

With a MIDI keyboard and software, we can play randomly pressed keys, producing notes until we hear a pattern that pleases us, and then record the tune with the MIDI software. We can adjust the notes, changing when they play and what they sound like, or change the tonal qualities, volume, and duration—all of it a practice of working the numbers that describe the experience. The benefit to us, as educators and learners, is that we can experience music as producers, without spending years of study and practice at mastering a single musical instrument.

To make things even more interesting, we can add additional note sets assigning different instruments. These are called tracks. We are stacking one instrument and its music on top of other instruments, resulting in an entire band—an entire orchestra.

Capturing play from a keyboard and editing the information with a computer mouse makes musical communication accessible to many more people than would have the opportunity in a world of only analog or acoustical instruments. It factors the music down to its component parts into a language that we can understand. The computer provides the interface whereby we can tweak the music and build the experience. Becoming good at it takes practice and, no doubt, an innate capacity to think musically. But it requires no more investment than many of us have already made with our home computers.

This does not mean that we will forget about traditional instruments or that fewer people will play them. Our high school bands are filled with teenagers investing enormous time and effort into mastering their instrument for the joy of performing big music to big audiences.

Employing Audio with Podcasting

Since the publishing of the first edition of this book, sound, as a form of communication, has become even more important and more prevalent in many classrooms around the world. Presentations about *podcasting* continue to be a major draw at educational technology conferences.

The term was probably coined in February of 2004 by Ben Hammersley, a reporter for *The Guardian*. In his article, "Audio Revolution," he interviewed Christopher Lydon, a journalist, who was working in Iowa reporting on the 2004 presidential primaries. He recorded his interviews with a portable digital audio recorder, saved them to his computer, and uploaded the audio files to a server on the Internet. Then he simply provided a link to the audio files from articles in his blog.

There was nothing new in this. People had been making audio and video files available to their information customers for many years. What made podcasting unique was that the RSS feed generated by the blog enabled

Lyon's listeners to subscribe to his reports using special aggregators. Each time he posted a new report, their aggregators were notified through the RSS feed, and the audio file was downloaded to their computer so that they could listen. If they used an iPod, then the file could be transferred to that portable audio device—the source of the term, podcasting.

Since then, classrooms around the world have not only been subscribing to education-related podcast programs, but also producing their own. Users of the iTunes software, available for both Mac and Windows computers, can browse through thousands of podcasts through the iTunes store and subscribe to their selections for free. If you own an iPod MP3 player, then you can configure iTunes to automatically transfer newly published podcast programs to your player.

The Education Podcast Network is another source for education-related podcasts. It provides access not only to podcasts that may be appropriate for listening by students, but also to 85 elementary school, 58 middle school, and 54 high school podcasts. These are audio and video programs that are produced mostly by students, learners who are developing skills in the literacy of employing audio (and video) information.

Podcasting is possibly one of the most accessible multimedia techniques available to classrooms. Many laptop computers have built-in microphones. External microphones are also available for as little as $20 or $30 (USD). Portable digital audio recorders can be purchased for as little as $50 (USD).

The fun part of podcasting, and the part that is most relevant to our examination of contemporary literacy, is what we can do with the audio file after it has been recorded. The audio of the podcast can be edited in a number of ways to add value to the message. Words can be deleted out, erasing the ubiquitous, "Ah," that permeates many monologs. Effects can be added to enhance and diminish various qualities of the recording. Additional sounds also can be added to enhance the sense of emotion and physical place. This kind of audio editing also can be easily and inexpensively achieved in most classrooms. A significant number of popular podcasts are produced using a free open source audio editing program called Audacity. Versions are available for both Windows computers and Mac OSX. Audacity is one of those unique programs that you can probably figure out how to use the first time you try it, but is so rich in features that you'll learn something new about it every time you use it.

Web Resource

Education Podcast Network - http://epnweb.org/

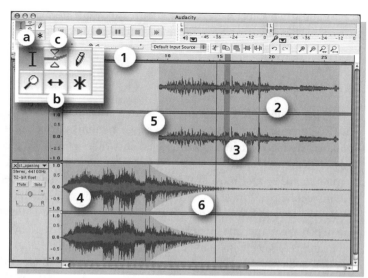

Figure 3.15: Audacity

This book is not supposed to be a how-to resource. But here is a very short tutorial on Audacity. Refer to Figure 3.15.

1. Assuming that we are using a laptop with a built-in microphone or a microphone connected to the computer, we press the red record button near (1) and start speaking, pressing the yellow square button to stop the recording.

2. The recording of our voice generates a track that illustrates the sound of our voice, labeled (2). Looking at the sound waves, we can distinguish individual words and syllables.

3. There is a misspoken word that we identify in the sound illustration. We use the Selection Tool (a), and highlight that word (3), using the tool, as if we were using a word processor. Then, as if we were using a word processor, we press **Delete** to remove the word.

4. To add some atmosphere to the spoken audio, we drop down the **Project** menu and select **Import Audio**. A file dialog box appears, and we select an audio MP3 file. It appears as a new track (4).

5. Because the music is playing at the same time as our spoke audio, we select the **Time Shift Tool** (b) and then grab the spoken track and move it further to the right (5), so that it will begin after some of the music has played.

Web Resource

Audacity - http://audacity.sourceforge.net/

6. Finally, we select the Envelop Tool (c) and squeeze the music track down, so that its volume declines as the spoken track begins (6).

Employing Video

I will spend quite a few pages on video production in the next chapter. It is a tool for communicating. But I want to suggest, in this chapter, that we start to think about video cameras in a different way. Although motion pictures have only been around for a very short 100 years, we have not known a world without them. Yet, for most of that time, sophisticated movie cameras and editing technologies have been the exclusive domain of marketing, entertainment, and news industries that paid for highly trained professional technicians and expensive, large, and complex technologies to produce their video communications. Today, with quality digital cameras available for as little as a hundred dollars and powerful editing software pre-installed on our computers, the reach and potential of these technologies are significantly expanded.

Our tendency, as a generation who has watched these technologies emerge, is to think about video in traditional terms. We think of studios, directors, scripts, and rehearsals. As a result we have established studios in our media centers and begun offering school news programming, sports event playbacks, and other imitations of our experiences with video. These are not bad uses of these tools, but we should realize and think about how the growing ubiquity of this technology will redefine how it is used.

> **Stop thinking about your school or classroom digital camera as a device for taking pictures. Instead, think of it as an input device.**

Stop thinking about your school or classroom digital camera as a device for taking pictures. Instead, think of it as an input device. Like a mouse, keyboard, or scanner, it is a device that allows us to capture information about the world around us and then input it into a computer. With the computer, we can manipulate, test, enhance, learn from, and better communicate the information. Traditional cameras are for recording images for later viewing. Digital cameras are for capturing visual information, so that we can do something with it.

As an example, several years ago, an educator was taking a walk through a neighborhood park. A medium-sized lake, which was part of the park, had become a winter refuge for sea gulls from the coast. Carrying a small video camera, he shot about 10 seconds of a large gull flying away from a bridge banister, provoked by the educator's approach. The grace of the animal was overwhelming. However, rather than simply watching the video upon return, he imported it into his computer, loading it into iMovie, where it became information to be employed.

iMovie features a number of special effects, including the ability to select a section of video and speed it up, or slow it down. The effect of viewing the bird flying, at speeds significantly slower than real life was, in a word, magnificent. We are able to see nuances of that bird's flight that we could not see without the computer. The educator was using the technique to employ that information to make visible that which was normally invisible.

We might also set the camera on a tripod and video a blooming flower or a tray of grass leaning toward light on the right, and then leaning back to a new light source on the left. After the video has been imported into the video editor, we could speed it up to dramatically illustrate motions of the plant world. Because motion can be captured and then edited/altered, we can employ that information to reveal what was initially invisible to the human eye, thereby employing information and exposing what is true.

Sources for Images to Employ

As we consider literacy in a rapidly changing information landscape, it is essential that we understand that this landscape is an environment of fertile content—information raw materials—that can be mined and employed to help us accomplish our goals. But there are many ethical issues to consider as we work the information, and these issues go further than just intellectual property. Many of these issues will be discussed in a later chapter. Information represents value and investment, and respecting that value and investment should be part of almost every lesson that we teach.

One of the best sources for images is Flickr. With both free and "Pro" services ($24.95/year for Pro), users of this Web tool can upload the digital photos they take on vacation, at weddings, birthday parties, holidays, and almost every other aspect of work and play. By uploading their photos, they are sharing visual information about their daily experiences to be seen and used by friends, family, neighbors, and the rest of the world. Flickr celebrated its two billionth photo upload in November 2007, receiving, at that time, 2.5 to 3 million new photos a day from people like you from almost all ages, walks of life, and parts of the world (Geoff).

It is important to note that because Flickr is a global service that relies on a community of users for its content, there are images that will be offensive to

Web Resource

Flickr http://flickr.com/

some people. But even if this site is blocked in your school, it remains a rich resource for educators as we plan our classroom activities and library centers away from the classroom. In addition, tools like Flickrstorm enable you to create sets of Flickr photos that you can bring into your school through the Web.

Flickr has addressed the issue of intellectual property by allowing photographers the choice of posting their images as rights-reserved or licensed using Creative Commons (CC). We will explore Creative Commons more in a later chapter, but this means that information consumers have more rights of use of the content, without permission, than with content that is copyrighted only.

Flickr also has enabled users to browse only images that are CC licensed by going to their creative commons Web search page. Here you can search photos based on the rights that the photographers have granted. See **Appendix D** for a brief description of each set of rights. It is enough to say that there are, at this writing, more than six-million searchable photos from this page that you are able to work in any way you wish, as long as you give credit to the original photographer.

Sources for Audio to Employ

People have been uploading audio into various archives and directories for years. Many have been commercialized, but there are still a variety of sites available with music and sound effects that are royalty free. With podcasting, the need arose for music that podcasters could use for their opening and closing segments. To fill that need, a number of podcast safe music sites appeared. They encourage musicians and composers, who do not want to commercialize their music or are looking for avenues to attract listeners, to make their work available for free to podcasters. A Google search for "podcast safe music" returns a number of these sites.

One of my favorite sources for audio sound effects is Partners in Rhyme. The site sells CDs of music and sounds, but also provides access to free and royalty free audio. Their sound effects page offers:

- Ambient sounds: weather, city sounds, crowd sounds

- Vehicle sounds: airplanes, cars, and hot rods

Web Resources

FlickrStorm http://zoo-m.com/flickr-storm/

Creative Commons http://creativecommons.org/

Flickr Creative Commons Images http://flickr.com/creativecommons/

Partners in Rhyme – http://partnersinrhyme.com/

- Human sounds: screams, applause, sports, and laughs

- General sounds: household, office, electric and door sounds, and

- Animal sounds: dogs barking, cats, big cats, safari animals, others.

The Internet Archive is another source for audio information. A search for speeches, in the audio section of their archive, returned 164 results, starting with the speeches of Lenin, the 100 best speeches of the United States, famous speeches of Malcolm X, and selected political speeches of the Weimar era from 1931.

Sources for Video to Employ

Sources for video content that can be employed are not as readily available, and having the rights to use the content are not as clear. But, there are places to go. For example, the Internet Archive, mentioned earlier in this chapter, offers a wealth of video and other multimedia content for employing. Most of the content is either public domain, licensed in the Creative Commons, or in some other licenses that at least allow its redistribution. Browsing the **Moving Images** section reveals sub-collections including:

- Animation and cartoons,

- Art and music,

- Computers and technology,

- Cultural and academic films,

- News and public affairs, and

- Youth media.

One source follows the same vein as Flickr. Even if you hadn't heard of Flickr, you probably know about YouTube, an archive of user-contributed video. Launched in February of 2005 by former PayPal employees, YouTube quickly became a major destination of Web users from around the world, ranked number three in traffic by Alexa's Global Top 100 ("Top Sites"). Lee Gomes, of the *Wall Street Journal*, reported in August 2006 that as of a month earlier, YouTube appeared to be hosting 5.1 million user uploaded videos. At the end of the month, that number had grown to 6.1 million videos, an increase of 20 percent. At this writing, a search of YouTube for "*" (a wildcard search) returned 62,800,000 hits.

> **Web Resource**
>
> YouTube - http://youtube.com/

YouTube does not currently allow users to download and edit video clips, though there are numerous tools available on the Net that will facilitate the retrieval and conversion from YouTube's Flash format. Many teachers use this capability so that they can bring instructionally selected video clips into their classrooms, when YouTube is blocked by their school's filtering software.

Employing RSS Feeds

We have already learned how RSS works and that we can use this powerful technique to train information to find us. However, we can also use RSS to mix content together into one place for others to use and enjoy. One example that utilizes some moderately sophisticated programming is Hitchhikr. This Web site enables conference planners and attendees to register upcoming events including dates, locations, descriptions, and suggested tags for bloggers and podcasters to use.

With the tags and other information entered into Hitchhikr, visitors who are interested in the 2008 National Educational Computing Conference (See Figure 3.16: Hitchhikr), can click it, and Hitchhikr looks to Flickr for blog entries tagged for the conference (Item 1), conducts a YouTube search for tagged videos (Item 2), and Flickr photos (Item 3). This tool employs metadata about user-generated content to create a single information product that brings it all together to one place.

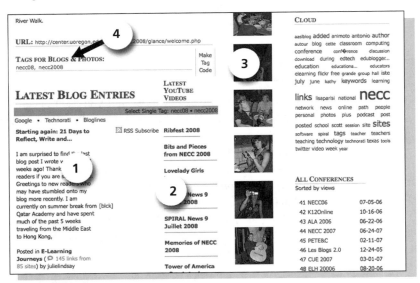

Figure 3.16: Hitchhikr

Web Resource

Hitchhikr - http://hitchhikr.com/

We have encountered this term, *tag*, several times already in this book. However, this is probably the best place to explain the concept, because it may have more to do with employing information, making it work for you, than any other aspect of contemporary literacy.

In a published print-based information environment, information products could easily be organized by placing them into labeled containers. Those containers may have been file folders and file cabinets, boxes, book shelves, or card catalog sets. When information is digital and networked, it becomes difficult to place it into a container. In fact, it is one of the significant qualities of today's information environment that content cannot be contained.

The solution came out of the library community and its efforts to use metadata as a way of organizing digital content. Metadata are information about the information, and when the information is digital, data about the data can be applied in a machine-readable format, such as XML. Computers can then organize the information for us and even mix with other information to add value.

A tag is a keyword that is applied to a digital information product, usually by the author or creator of the product—becoming part of the metadata about the product. In some cases, tags can be applied by the users of the product, as they sometimes find applications of the information that the author did not anticipate. Returning to Hitchhikr, the person who registers for a conference can suggest a tag to represent that conference. For instance, the person who submitted the 2008 National Educational Computing Conference suggested two tags for people who were generating information about the conference—bloggers and photographers. The tags were *necc08* and *necc2008* (See Item 4 in Figure 3.16: Hitchhikr). As a result, people who attended the conference and blogged about it, or took digital photos and uploaded them to Flickr, applied *necc2008* or *necc08* as tags for their information. The information could then be aggregated together on the Hitchhikr Web site.

This kind of aggregation of tagged information can be accomplished easily by educators and students using some Wiki tools. If you do not already have a Wiki page, you can set up a free site by visiting Wikispaces' teacher registration page and signing up as a teacher.

Web Resources

Wikispaces - http://wikispaces.com/
Wikispaces Teacher Registration - http://wikispaces.com/site/for/teachers100K/

As an example, you have been asked to provide some professional development for the teachers in your school regarding emerging technologies. Instead of creating a print handout that lists emerging tech resources on the Web, which will be up to date for about as long as it takes to get from the copier to the media center, you've decided to create a Web (Wiki) page that will list the latest in emerging technologies—and keeps updating this page as new sites are identified.

You might go to Delicious as a tool for keeping and organizing your bookmarks. As an ongoing process of storing the latest announcements and descriptions of emerging technologies, you have set up a tag labeled *emergingtech*, saving related Web sites under this tag, as they are discovered. When you login to Delicious, and your tags are listed, you can click *emergingtech* and receive a list of those sites, sorted from the most recent to the oldest.

At the bottom of that page, you find the RSS symbol. Right-click on the symbol (Mac users CTRL-Click), and copy the link location into you clipboard. The location of that RSS feed would look like this:

http://delicious.com/rss/(*your login*)/emergingtech

Go to your Wiki page and click on **Edit This Page**. Type in some sort of introduction, such as:

> The following Web sites describe technologies that are at varying stages of emergence. This list is dynamic. As new sites are discovered, they will be added here automatically. Please review these technologies periodically and reflect on how they might affect how and what we teach.

You can then click the Text Editor button and type the following code under your introduction:

[[rss url="" link="true" description="true" number="10" date="true"]]

Paste or type the URL of the Delicious RSS feed between the quotation marks after the URL, and then click to save the Wiki page. A listing of the latest 10 Web sites you have tagged with *emergingtech* and saved to Delicious will appear, including a hyperlink to the site, its description, and the date that it was added, as designated in the code above. If you would like to open the list up to anyone who is using Delicious and tagging sites with *emergingtech*, then you can replace *dwarlick* in the URL for the RSS feed with *tag*. This will list all Delicious sites tagged with *emergingtech*.

Figure 3.17 shows what the Web page will look like to the educators who attend your professional development.

The following web sites describe technologies that are at varying stages of emergence. This list is dynamic. As new sites are discovered, they will be added here automatically. Please review these technologies periodically and reflect on how they might affect how and what we teach.

Delicious/dwarlick/emergingtech

- ISTE | Emerging Technologies Database Jan 7, 2008 10:24 am
  ISTE's Emerging Technologies Task Force is increasing the educational community's knowl...
- article library : The Florida Files - Creative Class Group May 25, 2007 5:26 am
  The Creative Class Group (CCG) is a global think tank headquartered in Washington, DC that develo...
- informationfluency " home Apr 18, 2007 6:26 am
  Some fantastic resources from Joyce Valenza
- TEDTalks (audio, video) Jan 11, 2007 7:04 am
  Each year, TED hosts some of the world's most fascinating people: Trusted voices and convent...
- Untitled Document Dec 14, 2006 9:08 am
  Information and Community for Educators using M.U.V.E.'s
- ETech Conference 2007 • March 26-29, 2007 • San Diego, California Sep 25, 2006 3:34 pm
  When you say "sufficiently advanced technology" to a technologist, they'll invaria...
- alphaWorks : Emerging technologies Jun 15, 2006 6:23 pm
  The IBM Task Modeler is an Eclipse-based tool for rapidly creating and analyzing models of human ...
- EAF 228: Social Foundations of Education Jun 15, 2006 6:20 pm
  EAF 228 is an undergraduate, teacher education course designed as an online, interactive video ga...
- Pac Manhattan Jun 15, 2006 6:05 pm
  Pac-Manhattan is a large-scale urban game that utilizes the New York City grid to recreate the 19...
- IBM's 'Millipede' Project Demonstrates Trillion-Bit Data Storage Density Jun 15, 2006 6:05 pm
  Using an innovative nanotechnology, IBM scientists have demonstrated a data storage density of a ...

Figure 3.17: Wiki Aggregator

The difference between this technique and using an aggregator is that your aggregator is personal. You are training information to find you. Using the technique that we have just explored enables you to train categories of Web sites (or photos, news, and news searches, YouTube videos, others) to come to a page that you can make available to others—a new information document that is constantly republished based on employing information well beyond your physical control. Employing the information.

Employing the Web (Mashups)

Mashups are showing up in a variety of information venues, including video, music, and Web development. Simply put, a mashup is an information product that has been constructed, at least partly, by mixing portions of other information products together to form something of value or enjoyment. Music mashups consist of tunes or songs where portions of other music or sounds are mixed together using audio or music editing software. Video mashups are mixes of other video clips such as speeches, news clips, commercials, scenes from popular movies, or other sources.

These media mashups are typically constructed for entertainment and shared within social networks or in user submitted venues like YouTube. At this writing, a search of YouTube for "*mashup*" returned 39,800 videos. Conversations about the copyright implications of assembling mashups continues, though a growing source of information raw materials are emerging out of the Creative Commons community. Still, much of the entertainment of media mashups is in recognizing the bits and pieces that make up the message.

Web Mashups

Some talented programmers and resourceful tech educators also have used the World Wide Web to generate mashups. Typically, this involves tricking the capabilities of one Web site, along with unrelated information either added in or accessed (or scraped) in from other Web pages, combining the information to create a new and valuable Web service.

In January 2008, David Jakes constructed a mashup between information about the JFK assassination and a Google Streetview stroll. Jakes utilized Google maps, inserting a trail in downtown Dallas, Texas, following the route that President John Kennedy's motorcade took on November 22, 1963. The Mashup sets Google in Streetview mode where we find ourselves standing on Elm Street able to move up or down the route. We can also use the mouse to look up at the Texas Textbook Depository, where the shots that killed President Kennedy were fired, allegedly, by Lee Harvey Oswald. These types of mashup tours are not difficult for teachers or even students to prepare.

To further mix things up, Jakes created a narrated walk through using Camtasia screen casting software and created a demo page on Screencast. You can view the demonstration at:

http://screencast.com/users/djakes/playlists/Google%20Streetview/

Buzztracker, one of my favorite Web mashups, was developed by a team of writer/publishers in Japan. The site scrapes news data from Google News and mixes it with mapping software, written by the team, to generate a world map that illustrates where news is happening at any moment, how much news is happening there, and other locations that are related.

Archived pages are also available. Students can see where news was happening on specific dates by employing the following URL, editing the dates and loading the pages:

http://buzztracker.org/2008/01/03/index.html

Web mashups are created by talented and creative people with both basic and deep technology skills. The ability to create mashups is not, yet, a basic

Web Resources
Google Streetview - http://maps.google.com/
Camtasia - http://techsmith.com/
Screencast - http://screencast.com/
Buzztracker - http://buzztracker.org/

literacy skill. But it is important that students, who are becoming literate in today's information environment, learn how that environment can be worked—that it can be employed to add value.

You can learn more about Web mashups and explore a growing database of sites at Programmable Web.

Machinima

Machinima is a treat and one of the most intriguing applications of today's information landscape to emerge in recent years. It works like this:

1. A teenager plays a Massively Multi Player Online Roll Playing Game (MMORPG), such as Halo or World of Warcraft. Friends from nearby, or from far away, are playing together in the virtual game environment.

2. Our teenager has connected her game system to her computer, in much the same way that we might connect our video camera to a computer. As a result, the game play can be viewed on the computer's display.

3. But rather than playing the game, the teens are acting. Someone has written a script. They have rehearsed and are acting out a story in the game environment.

4. Using video editing software (iMovie on a Mac or MovieMaker on a Windows computer), the teenager captures the virtual performance as a video file.

5. The leader then uses the video editing software to refine the performance, add in music and special effects, titles, and credits.

Machinima is a blend of the words *machine* and *cinema* and involves using digital editing software to capture video from games and other virtual environments. The video is then edited with other content to tell a story. It represents one more example of how content today has become a raw material. For a small but influential percentage of today's youngsters, this concept of "information as raw material" has become a central feature of their information environment and experience, and this continues to challenge our notions about literacy.

Perhaps the best source for information about a technique that is so new is Wikipedia's Machinima page. You can also view thousands of machinima products by searching for YouTube videos tagged with *machinima*.

Web Resources

Programmable Web - http://programmableweb.com/

Wikipedia's Machinima Page - http://en.wikipedia.org/wiki/Machinima

YouTube Videos tagged with machinima - http://youtube.com/results?search_query=machinima&search=tag

Conclusion

In the 20th century, we were taught to work information by math teachers. In most other classes under most circumstances, information was a product to simply be consumed, learned, and then reported back on tests. In the 21st century, we will all be working with information, and not all of that information will be numbers on a sheet of paper. Often, they are going to be the ones and zeros embedded in a universe of digital content. For this reason, we must change our notions about the skills that we teach, expanding the range of information processing skills well beyond the traditional standards of arithmetic. Being able to add, subtract, count, measure, calculate, and manipulate numbers will remain a prerequisite for being literate in the 21st century. However, for today's information-driven technology-rich world, students must learn to process the numbers that are embedded in all information.

These skills will be as critical to their future as the ability to count.

Action Items

Directors of Technology

- Emphasize the use of productivity tools in your technology program (word processing, spreadsheets, databases, graphics, music, and video production). Offer professional development accordingly.

- Establish an annual technology fair for your district. Feature booths where teachers and students demonstrate their digital work and discuss what they learn and teach in the process. Include booths where students demonstrate what they are doing with information outside of class (mashups and machinima).

- Establish a district mailing list or social network where teachers can share and discuss how they are employing digital information and teaching these concepts and skills to their students.

- Consider forming professional learning communities about teaching with digital content, where educators can share and teach each other about the techniques they are learning and then share the skills and products more broadly with the district.

- Create a district museum of student-constructed information products organized by subject area. This can be a video exhibit at the district office or a Web site.

- Create or participate in a social archive of teacher created and contributed learning objects and resources, and promote it as a collaborative tool for all teachers.

- Consider sharing videos of students and teachers employing information with other educators through the Professional Development channel of TeacherTube or with the community through YouTube.

Principals

- When delivering performance and demographic data to teachers for use in planning, demonstrate how the data are employed to tell a story about your school, its strengths, weaknesses, and other characteristics.

- During evaluations, ask teachers how they are using digital information in their lessons, and the techniques they are using to add value to the information. Ask to see examples.

- Ask how their students are using digital information, how they are working the information, and what they are learning. Ask to see examples.

- Purchase digital still and video cameras so that any teacher can make use of the technology at any time. Work toward providing a still and video camera for each classroom. Consider purchasing boxes of inexpensive digital cameras so that students can use them to capture, work, and express ideas visually.

- Consider purchasing one or more music production stations for the school library. Invite students to play and then share what they learn from their play.

- Consider starting a school podcast that features interviews with teachers and students, and examples of new and exciting content-working activities in your classrooms.

- Establish a section of the school's Web site for showcasing student and teacher productions.

Media Specialists

- Introduce teachers and students to Creative Commons and help them to start licensing their content using the technique.

- Establish a digital library of student produced (CC licensed) digital products: reports, Web pages, images, tunes, and video. Make these products available to other students for reference and as information raw materials for future work.

- Make sure that computer work stations in your media center all give students access to productivity tools (word processing, spreadsheets, graphics, music, and video production), and staff to support students in its use.

- Set up one or more production stations equipped with scanner, digital microscope, interfaces for connecting to handheld devices, and other input peripherals.

- Set up one or more music production stations in your media center, including keyboard, drum machine, and music software.

- Coordinate with art, music, drama, media, and technology education classes to support their programs. Promote your media center as a workshop for these classes.

- Set up one or more computers in the media center as a display station for showcasing digital products created by students or teachers.

- Help establish and support professional learning communities among teachers who want to learn more and share what they are learning about teaching in the digital information landscape.

- Continue to promote your media center as a place to find answers and solutions. But also start to promote it as a place to come and work the information. Think *Kinko's for Kids*.

School Tech Facilitators

- Map the school's curriculum in a way that you and the media specialist have access to what is currently being taught by each teacher. Use this information to suggest ways for teachers and students to employ digital information for teaching and learning.

- Offer ongoing professional development in the use of productivity software (word processing, spreadsheets, databases, graphics, music, and video production) for creating digital products.

- Assist technology director in promoting and supporting a social archive of teacher constructed and contributed digital learning objects and resources.

- Explore ways that scientists, engineers, and business people employ information in their work. Look closely at scientific computation, using computers to visualize large amounts of data and share what you learn with your school.

Teachers

- Take every opportunity to play with your computer. Play around with spreadsheets. Take some pictures and load them into a graphics program and just start clicking buttons to observe the effects. Share what you learn.

- Identify the students in your classroom who are already adept at using productivity software. Ask for their advice on an ongoing basis, even if the information is not digital.

- Think of the computer as a laboratory. Create a spreadsheet with demographic information or scientific observations, and ask students to learn something from it. Use your class experts as consultants.

- While you teach science and history, teach how scientists and historians (and others) do their job using digital information. Do not just teach science. Teach students how to be scientists.

- Note those students who do not have easy access to technology outside of the classroom, and explore ways of getting it to them through the school tech facilitator, media specialist, principal, and district offices.

- Consider forming a casual professional learning community of other teachers interested in building their digital content skills and sharing with other educators. Meet regularly for pizza or coffee and share. Many pizza and coffee establishments now offer wireless access to the Internet.

Students

- Play with your computers. I know that this is like telling a fish to swim, but take advantage of the time you have. It is your one advantage over us.

- If you are using a social network, explore what other people are doing, and if it's special, ask them how they accomplished this.

- Suggest extra-credit assignments that you can perform by analyzing or manipulating data.

- If you do not understand a concept, process, or other piece of knowledge, ask your teacher to show you a picture, a video, or a diagram.

- When appropriate, ask your teacher how a real scientist does this, or a real historian, health worker, politician, or mathematician.

Parents

- Make sure that each of your children has access to a computer connected to the Internet. This does not mean that each child should have her own computer, but that she has reasonable access.

- Install productivity software on your home computer(s). This would include word processing, spreadsheets, graphics software, and music and video production. Especially cater to special interests of your children (art, music, photography, writing).

- If your job involves employing information in some way, explain it to your children. If possible, take them to your workplace and demonstrate. Explain what you have to know and the experience you need in order to perform this task.

CHAPTER 4

Expressing Ideas Compellingly

A s youngsters, many of us played little league baseball. Very few were really good at it. We all understood, though, that the most glamorous position on the baseball team was the pitcher. Even though being a catcher was also cool, because of the gear you got to wear, the pitcher was the one player whom everyone watched on every play.

His job was to use velocity and spin, and a certain amount of psychology, to get the ball past the batter. If the batter saw through the psychology, was able to compensate for the angle, and match the velocity, then he connected with the ball and stood a chance of being the hero.

Baseball is not as much a sport of choice for today's children. They play soccer and compete on the swim team. So today, more often than not, when someone talks about pitching, it has to do with pitching an idea, convincing someone to accept your vision and help you accomplish your goal. The pitcher still uses velocity, spin, and psychology to make the pitch, but the goal is to help the receiver connect, not to get the idea past him. As more and more of the manufacturing of our products is automated, people will spend their time dealing with the information that drives the production, distribution, sales, and support: programming, inventory planning, marketing, and the systems that provide the structure for supporting it all. Success and prosperity will depend less on natural resources, and more on the development and crafting of that information infrastructure—and the communication that happens within it. Systems will compete with other systems, and success will depend on the quality of the information and its presentation.

Our personal shopping is increasingly based on information. We shop from home, in front of a computer, browsing through Web sites, comparing information—not the actual products—packaged on the shelf. In the Information Age, information will compete for attention in much the same way that products on a store shelf competed for attention during the Industrial Age.

One of the most important reasons that we communicate is to affect the behavior of other people. You want someone to have a higher regard for you. You may want someone to pick your plan for improvement over that of a competitor or colleague. You may want to affect the voting behavior of constituents, homework habits of your students, or buying habits of consumers. These are all accomplished by expressing ideas not only clearly, but also compellingly.

> " In the Information Age, information will compete for attention in much the same way that products on a store shelf competed for attention during the Industrial Age. "

This is old news for educators. Our job is to sell ideas, to affect what students know, believe, and can do. We do this not by simply delivering content, but by creating and crafting messages and information experiences that cause students to gain the knowledge that is required. In recent years we have learned more about how people think and learn. As a result, we have improved our techniques for helping our students gain knowledge and skills by delivering messages in a variety of ways. This is a realization that we should impart to our students, because they will all become teachers, and for that they will need powerful communication skills.

Communicating Compellingly—Text

Traditionally, we have taught writing as a communication skill. We have helped students to learn the rules of grammar and syntax, punctuation, and spelling. Many of us have even helped students learn to be good writers, able to influence and entertain other people with their words. This will not end. As the director Martin Scorsese says, ". . . whatever cinema evolves into, you will still need an author."

As we reflect on recent technological changes in communication, it is important that we think about the effects that these new tools may have on the quality of written communication. At a recent meeting of technology-savvy educators, the suggestion arose that we allow students to use instant messaging software in the classroom in order to conduct collaborative and cooperative learning activities. One teacher immediately asked, "How do we assure that the students will be practicing good writing while they are messaging instead of all of those shortcuts?" Other educators in the room nodded their heads in agreement, and the idea was dropped.

We should not feel challenged by these new ways of communication. In fact, it might be more appropriate to be in awe. These children, as a generation, have invented a new grammar specifically designed for a communication avenue that will almost certainly be a part of their future. We should respect this and even marvel at how well these kids have adapted a new tool to their tasks and lifestyle and to enriching their personal relationships. Their new grammar is not intended to replace the old, but to serve a unique purpose. At the same time that we teach them the grammar of formal writing, we should respect their language and even be willing to ask them to teach it to us. (See Figure 4.1: IM Speak)

Traditionally, we have taught writing through avenues that are fairly artificial and specific to the academic arena. We have asked students to write essays, themes, and research papers. Creativity and innovation expert, Sir Ken Robinson says,

> If you were to visit education as an alien and say what's it for, public education, I think you'd have to conclude, if you look at the output, who really succeeds by this, who does everything they should, who gets all the brownie points, who are the winners, I think you'd have to conclude the whole purpose of public education throughout the world is to produce university professors. (Robinson)

" **To teach students to write compellingly, we must give them compelling reasons to write.** "

Outside of school, we write letters, reports, e-mail messages, and persuasive copy that are aimed at influencing other people. To teach students to write compellingly, we must give them compelling reasons to write. Students should produce authentic information products aimed at real audiences with meaningful goals in mind. This is not as difficult as it might seem. There are models out there, though not in the arena of writing instruction.

If you have been teaching for more than 15 years, you may have taken vocational education classes when you were in school. They may have included industrial arts, drafting, and a number of clerical courses. At that time, they were quite relevant subjects as there were probably more employment opportunities in industrial fields. The assignments that came out of those

Instant Messaging Grammar (R. Warlick)

Participating in an Instant Messaging conversation (IM'ing) requires agreed upon conventions in order to communicate effectively and efficiently. Two rules that seem to underlie IM communication is that capital letters serve to increase the auditory volume of the conversation. In other words you capitalize in order to shout, and this is considered rude in most circumstances. So all text is generally in lower case. Shift keys also slow you down.

Secondly, IM'ers do not use punctuation, except for commas, which they find to be indispensable. Again, extra keys slow you down and they are all in difficult to reach positions.

IM'ing makes extensive use of abbreviations and a series of punctuations to simulate facial expressions, emoting gestures of emotion.

Abb.	Explanation
:-)	Happy face
;-)	Winking happy face
:-(	Sad face
^_^	Happy anime face
bbl	Be Back Later
bc	Because
brb	Be Right Back
btw	By The Way
grrrr	Growl, expression of anger
hw	HomeWork
im	Instant Messager
jk	Just Kidding
K	oK!
lmao	Laugh My Ass Off
lol	Laughing Out Loud
nmh	Not Much Here
nmu	Not Much, yoU?
o	Oh
omg	Oh My Gosh (form of exclamation)
r	aRe
sn	Screen Name
sp	previous word may be misSPelled
sup	what'S UP?
thankz	thank you
ttfn	Ta Ta For Now!
ttyl	Talk To You Later
u	yoU
ur	yoUR/you're

Figure 4.1: IM Speak

Inventing an Authentic Assignment

Task	Example
1. Who, in the adult world, would have a stake in this topic?	Geography is the topic. One profession that would be interested in this topic is a travel agent.
2. What kind of information product might this person use or create?	The travel agent would use and, in many cases, create travel brochures.
3. What would be the value of the information product? What goals would it help accomplish?	The goal of the travel brochure would be to convince people that they should travel to a specific place.
4. What specific information would be required to accomplish the goal and what would be the best way for that information to convey itself?	Geographic and culture facts, pictures, video clips, quotes for people who have been there or people living there.

Assignment:	Ask students to work in teams to produce a travel brochure to New Zealand and include in the evaluation rubric a provision that determines the persuasiveness of the product.

Figure 4.2: Authentic Assignment

classes were different in nature from those that you received in academic classes. They involved the design or construction of products that people might actually use. There was an authentic audience and an authentic goal for the work. The teacher did not simply deliver content, but served as a consultant or facilitator, helping us to ask the right questions, and to make decisions regarding technique, materials, and tools. In the industrial age, this type of teaching, in industrial arts classes, made perfect sense. In the information age, it makes just as much sense to teach information arts classes in exactly the same way.

Devising authentic assignments is different from traditional ones, but it is not difficult. See Figure 4.2 for steps in crafting authentic writing assignments.

When potential customers shop online, they are comparing information rather than comparing the actual product. In order to be successful, the information must compete for the attention of those customers.

Expressing Text Compellingly

Information must communicate itself as clearly and efficiently as possible. This is a concept that we have come to realize with the advent of the World Wide Web. For the earliest Web publishers, Web development was largely a technical endeavor. You learned HTML (HyperText Markup Language) in order to create hyperlinks between documents and to accomplish some basic formatting of the information. But hyperlinks, not formatting, were the great benefit of the Web, the ability to connect similar and supporting documents together—creating a web of information. As new features like tables, animated GIFs, and frames became available, they were considered enhancements that we used with little regard other than demonstrating our own technical chops. Unfortunately, these formatting enhancements frequently rendered our information useless as they distracted attention away from the message rather than improve it.

As we started using our Web log files (statistics on how people use the Web site) and saw that an enormous and growing number of people were actually looking at our pages, we began to pay attention to what the viewers of our pages were actually doing with the information, how these visits were helping them, and how they were helping us. We became more interested in how the information communicated itself. We began to tone down the frames and animated GIFs, and to hide our use of tables for information layout. We also began to look at Web publishing as a way to accomplish our goals by influencing other people. We began to communicate. If information is competing for attention, then we must learn to package the information in much the same way that we package products for the store shelf. While we fill our pages with pictures and paragraphs of coherent and compelling text, we must consider the various levels in which people access information. For instance, what do they learn from a document upon first glance? Usually, when people consider a document, they subconsciously ask:

- How much time will I have to invest in this document?

- How likely is it to include the answer to my question or problem?

- How much am I going to have to work, intellectually, to understand this information?

- Will my time be better spent continuing my search for a better document?

- Information that successfully competes for attention will help readers start answering these questions before they even start to read.

Figure 4.3 illustrates a few rules that you might consider when developing a report, project description, handout, work sheet, or when evaluating your students' information products.

Regardless of whether students are producing a written report, Web page, picture, multimedia presentation, or software, communication needs to become a core part of its evaluation. Consider including at least one element in your evaluation rubrics that asks how well the student has arranged the information for communication. (See Figure 4.4: Communication Rubric)

Objective	Below Standard	Standard	Above Standard
Evidence that author is attentive to information layout to improve communication	No evidence that the author has considered information layout to improve communication.	Some elements of the document illustrate concious decisions on the arrangement of information to improve its communication.	The document illustrates concious and persistant attention to information layout to improve education.

Figure 4.4: Communication Rubric

In addition, if the assignment has an authentic audience, there may be a way to establish authentic assessment. Several years ago, The Landmark Project ran an online project called Eco-Entrepreneur. Classes on the Internet were asked to form teams of students in mock companies. Each company was tasked with using their imaginations to devise a brand new product that they believed people their own age would want to buy. They had to develop the concept of their product to a point where they could write a successful sales pitch.

Packaging Information

Less is Better
After writing your text, go back and identify every word or phrase that does not help you deliver your message or goal. Then delete it. You will find that you can lose as much as half of your text when you do this.

Short Paragraphs
Presenting text in six short paragraphs with white space between looks like reading then presenting two or three long paragraphs. Try to keep paragraphs down to three or four sentences each.

Traditional Text

Hanging Indents
Headings and subheadings should be flush to the left of the page margin. The content should be indented. The hanging headings make the document easier to scan.

Bold Important Words and Phrases
Select words and phrases that will be of special interest to the reader or that help you draw their attention to the information you want them to read. Bold these words to create eye magnets, so that the scanning reader will easily find them.

Packaged Text

Bullet Lists
Any list of more than two items should be bulleted. A bulleted or numbered list is easier to read, study and learn. A list is a specific type of information and it should be distinguished from prose.

Use Font and Style Changes
Your document may include several types of information, such as: descriptions, instructions, captions or lists. These various types of information are read in different ways. It should be clear to the reader, at a glance, when information type has changed. One way to do this is by changing the text's font, size, indentation, or style.

Use Appropriate Media
Many concepts can be more easily expressed and understood as graphical images, such as graphs, tables, or diagrams. If a concept can be expressed as a graphic organizer, it usually communicates better that way.

Figure 4.3: Format Rules

After they wrote their sales pitch, it was uploaded to a Web site where the text became part of a simulated online catalog. Participating classes were asked to visit the online catalog and students were asked to select the items they would buy, with a specified amount of money on hand. These mock orders were recorded on the site where the company teams could monitor sales.

The primary instructional objective of the activity was to help students develop persuasive writing skills. The students evaluated their own work by watching how others responded. The more clear, easy-to-understand, and persuasive their writing, the more orders they received. If teams found that their products were not being ordered, they could refine their sales pitches, re-install them, and continue to watch for orders. Assessment was built-in.

New Opportunities for Expressing Text

Blogging

Although there was a bourgeoning community of bloggers when the first edition of this book was published, it was on the radar of only a handful of educators. It was at the 2004 National Educational Technology Conference (NECC), in New Orleans, that master edublogger, Will Richardson, introduced us to the practice and its instructional potentials. At that time, Richardson was a high school teacher, and all of his students had their own blogs. At the conference, he told compelling stories about a new kind of student learning that stemmed more from conversation than from just writing. Since 2004, blogging has spread to schools around the world as a way of giving voice to student learning, to empower them to share their knowledge and understanding, and engage in knowledge-building conversations.

At least part of the reason for the growth of education blogging, or edublogging, is its simplicity. The diagram in Figure 4.5 traces a process that is, at a fairly basic level, about literacy. Reading clockwise from the top, the blogger reads, reflects, writes, refines, and then publishes her ideas. Readers then read her article, reflect, write, refine, and publish comments. The blogger reads the comments, reflects, writes, refines, and posts another comment. It is in this cycle that the value of blogging happens from a literacy point of view. It becomes a conversation requiring that people read, reflect, and write, all within a community. Writing stops being about writing and it becomes a communication assignment.

Web Resources

Will Richardson's Blog - http://weblogg-ed.com/

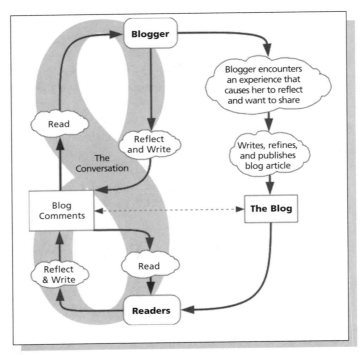

Figure 4.5: Blogging

Traditional writing assignments tend to make only one cycle. The student's work goes to the teacher, who assesses the writing according to instructional expectations, and then a grade is returned to the student. Multiple cycles occur when students are blogging their assignments with multiple participants. An assignment can take on a life of its own, and this, like this emerging new information landscape, can be exciting.

There are a variety of blogging services available today that are designed specifically for classrooms. They include:

- IMBEE—http://imbee.com/
- ePals—http://epals.com/
- Gaggle—http://gaggle.net/
- 21 Classes—http://21classes.com/
- Class Blogmeister—http://classblogmeister.com/

Wikis and Other Collaborative Writing Tools

Wikis are typically not as focused on compelling communication as blogging and other forms of publishing. Instead, they involve a small community of people (students, teachers, administrators) who are collaborating to produce a document that will be useful to that small group of people. The diagram in

Figure 4.6 describes a community of four people who are each contributing to and reading from a common Wiki page.

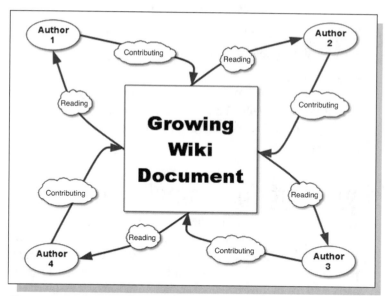

Figure 4.6: Wiki Diagram

Each of the four authors has access to the Wiki page for reading. Each author also has a password that allows him to edit the Wiki page with a click of the **Edit this Page** line, entering his password, and then editing the document in a way that will add value. Many collaborative Wikis become reference works that the users can continue to depend on. In these instances, the communication has less to do with its ability to compel, and is more about the layout and organization.

One professional use of a Wiki might be a secondary school discipline department, where the teachers collaborate on a common Wiki document to describe and continually adapt their curriculum. They use this tool to update and refine their standards, instructional techniques, and resources. The focus of idea expression shifts from being compelling to being practical. The text and images must be written and arranged in a way that makes the document useful to the community.

Many teachers are requiring students to create and maintain their own study guides for their units of instruction. The students task themselves not only with recording the best information, but also with organizing the information so that it can be studied easily. To make their work more authentic, the entire class might be open to use any of the student-produced study guides, with extra points going to the team whose guide receives the most visits, or who produces the most used/useful document.

There are three major Wiki tools that are used by classrooms today. They are:

- Wikispaces—http://wikispaces.com/

- PBWiki—http://pbwiki.com/

- Wetpaint—http://wetpaint.com/

Google provides a service that is similar to Wikis in some important ways. Google Docs offers a Web-based word processor that allows communities of people to work together on the same document. One of the interesting features of Google Docs is that more than one person can edit the document at the same time.

Communicating Compellingly—Images

When packaging information that competes for attention, it is important to decide what kind of voice will best communicate the message. Often, this will be text. Words communicate precisely, and can evoke imagination and passion. However, information can frequently communicate itself more fully and clearly with images. For example, if students are assigned to create a field trip brochure to be used to introduce next year's class to the trip, even the most talented writers will not be able to portray the experience of that museum, historic park, or municipal institution as well as a vivid and descriptive picture. This is one reason why every classroom should have access to digital still cameras. Pictures communicate rich information that can be easily grasped by the viewer, because images are a language that all brains are wired to understand. Yet, creating a picture that communicates requires skill no less sublime than learning to write.

When students take pictures with a digital camera or produce images with a graphics program or colored pencils, they should be encouraged to use the picture to deliver a message or to tell a story. Students should be asking these questions, "What do I want to accomplish with this picture?" "What story am I trying to tell?" These questions should be at the core of the assignment.

One way to help students learn to think about pictures as a communication device is to have them try to tell the stories of pictures they encounter around them. As an example, you might take a photograph or painting from a historic event that students are studying. Ask students to list what they see in the picture. They will list the obvious items of the picture. Next, divide the picture vertically and horizontally, into four quadrants, and then ask teams of students to identify what they see in only one quadrant. Here they will see things that were not apparent when looking at the whole picture. Ask the teams to list both physical items and actions that they see in the picture quadrants. The story of the picture will manifest itself in more detail. Finally, ask students how the less obvious elements they see contribute to the overall story or message. Giving students this kind of image reading (literacy) practice will help them to think about the pictures they are producing as avenues of communication.

The National Archives & Records Administration Web site includes many digital sources for pictures and worksheets that will help students learn to read images and other media, and, ultimately, how to communicate.

Teachers and Images

Think of your classroom digital camera as an everyday tool of expression. Also, think of it as a note-taking tool. Carry it around in your pocket. When you see students successfully accomplishing something that they have been working hard for, take a picture. Digital cameras are a way of collecting information. If you are giving homework assignments, and routinely write them on the board, take a picture of the board notes every day, and post that picture on your classroom Web page. Save yourself some time. If we, as teachers, come to realize the communication power of our images, we can begin to teach it to our students.

Make yourself familiar with sources for images. With each lesson, look for images that might communicate more effectively. If an image communicates a concept, it may be the best way to communicate that idea. If you are producing a set of presentation slides for your class, rely on images as much as you possibly can. A bulleted list is a sign that you failed to find a better way of conveying your topic, or you just didn't try.

There are many sources for images to use in your lessons. The Web site for this book includes a dynamic listing. Some of the obvious include:

- Flickr—http://flickr.com/
- Google Image Search—http://images.google.com/
- Library of Congress—http://loc.gov/
- Smithsonian Institute—http://si.edu/

Students and Images

Ask students to express what they are learning with pictures. A teacher in North Carolina recently asked students to use their digital cameras to

Web Resources

National Archives & Records Administration - http://archives.gov/education
Redefining Literacy - http://davidwarlick.com/redefining_literacy

express their vocabulary words with pictures. They used inexpensive cameras (less than $100) to walk around in their classroom and photograph objects that reminded them of their assigned vocabulary word. With this near ubiquitous access to image recording and production technology, students learned to express what they were studying with images, and, as a result, to think harder about what they were learning. The teacher reported that the first week she used this technique, the students' vocabulary quiz scores skyrocketed.

Layers	Layers enable you to divide your image into elements that can be manipulated independently and stacked in a variety of ways.
Resizing	Often you need to make your picture larger or smaller. Consider that making a picture larger can result in loss of quality.
Save As (file types)	You can save an image as a variety of file types. TIF and EPS files produce high quality printings. JPG and GIF files work best on the Web.
Tools	Some of the most common and useful tools include: Marquee & Lasso – Enables you to select and capture sections of the image Paint Brush – Enables you to mark your image in a variety of ways by layer Eraser – Will erase sections of your image by layer Text – Allows you to include typed text in your images Shapes – Enable you to add rectangles and circles to your image Eye Dropper – Click a spot on your image, and the color of that spot will be adopted as the default color in your palette Zoom – Usually a magnifying glass icon, this tool enables you to enlarge specific sections of the image for more refined work
Copy and Paste	Elements of an image can be selected (with the marquee or lasso), copied, and pasted onto other images or into specific layers of an image.
Cropping	This enables you to select the most important section of your picture and then remove all outlying sections.

Figure 4.7: Graphics Features

We can also build images using graphics software or enhanced photographs to clarify our message. We explored a number of tools in the previous chapter about employing information. Figure 4.7 lists just a few of the features that can be employed in image editing software to more compellingly express our ideas.

Graphics Software

Cropping Frequently, the picture that you start with has more information on it than you need. Information that does not help you accomplish your goal will distract you from your goal. This can often be solved by cropping out the unwanted part of the image. To do this, use the marquee selector to select only the part of the image you want to keep and then select **Crop** from the **Image** menu.

Marquee

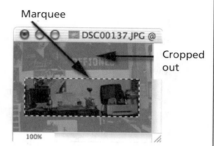

Cropped out

Clouding This is another technique for drawing attention to an image. In order to make the focal point of the image part of the document you can use the **Eraser** tool of the graphics program, set to **Air Brush** mode, and erase out the surrounding part of the image. This gives a much softer version of the image, making it appear out of the document, rather than stamped onto the page.

Using the eraser to wash out unwanted parts of the image.

Its appearance within the document

Layering This is one of the most powerful features of graphics software. In a sense, layering allows you to placed a sheet of glass over the picture and then paint on the glass. Anything that you paint on the glass will not affect the original image. The glass or layer can be moved around for position. Additional layers can be added creating any number of pictures that stack on top of each other making a single picture. I frequently add layers in order to label a picture. In the example to the right each label is a separate layer allowing them to be positioned to most effectively communicate.

Computer for gaming, research, and homework.

TV for Cable programming and gaming

Handheld video game.

Video game controller.

Figure 4.8: Editing an Image

Figure 4.8 illustrates a number of techniques that can be used to more compellingly express our messages with pictures.

To help them learn to communicate with pictures, ask students to do just that—communicate with each other. Images can easily be posted on student blogs, where classmates can critique the pictures through their comments. Here are a few ideas for activities that ask students to communicate with pictures.

- Give students a list of quotes from literature they are reading. Ask teams (or individuals) to produce a single picture that portrays the idea of the quote. Then ask the entire class to match the pictures with the quotes. If they get it right, you did a good job of communicating.

- After teaching a concept in math, ask students to produce a picture that illustrates how or why the concept might be used outside of the classroom.

- Ask students to list things they do every day. Then ask them to produce a set of pictures that will provide instructions on how to perform one of the tasks. Allow the students to include words in their images, but limit the number of words they can use. For example, "You can include up to 10 words in your picture."

- If students are studying a historic controversy, or one in current events, ask them to use existing pictures from the Internet to produce a montage that exemplifies one of the positions involved in the controversy.

- Ask students to take or produce pictures that illustrate the effects of good or bad health habits.

- If students are producing a presentation for a report, limit the number of words that they are allowed to use.

Communicating Compellingly—Animation

Pictures tell stories by standing still. Animation tells a story by moving, showing the difference between one moment and another—a previous condition compared with the result of an action. We see animation almost everywhere. It has become an integral part of television communication. Spend a half hour with the nightly news and count the number of times that the report utilizes animation. Watch a five-minute weather report and count. Increasingly we are seeing animation on flat screen video monitors in stores, elevators, airports, and at gas pumps. The reason that we are seeing so many animated images is because they communicate very well. They tell a story. We are a species that is wired-up to time, and comparing one moment to the next is a big part of how we view and understand our world. Once again, communication is a process of helping other people to understand our world.

Flash

There are four ways of producing animations in the classroom that are relatively practical. The first, and probably least accessible to most schools, is Flash, a product and technology from Adobe. This is a sophisticated type of animation that is especially powerful because the user's mouse can interact with the animation, enabling customized actions, branching, and even simulations. Flash is not for every teacher or every school. However, many teachers have learned to use it, and some even produce sophisticated instructional animations for their students. The downside is that Flash authoring is fairly expensive, and learning to produce Flash animations requires a learning curve for most people.

In recent years a number of options have emerged that make this powerful form of animation a little more accessible. Projects include Ajax Animator, SWFTools, and SWFMill. In addition, Impress, the presentation portion of OpenOffice (an open source productivity suite similar to Microsoft Office) will output presentation slides as Flash files. Later versions of Apple's Keynote presentation software will also export slides as Flash files.

GIF Animations

Another more accessible form of animation is GIF animations. A GIF is a type of image file that is frequently used on Web pages. An animated GIF is a single image file that stacks numerous images in layers on top of each other. In a sense, an animated GIF acts like a digital flipbook that plays the individual GIF images in sequence. If each image is a slightly altered version of the previous image, then the effect is motion or animation. For instance, I might use my graphics program to produce an image with the words *Express* and *Yourself*, each in a separate layer. I save the image as file1.gif and then move the two words (layers) a little closer together. Then I save the picture again, this time as file2.gif. I continue this process until I have adjusted and saved the file 10 times (file1.gif to file10.gif). Arranged around, they might look like Figure 4.9.

I can then run a freeware program that can be downloaded from the Internet called *GifBuilder*, and load the 10 individual images into the software. There are a number of parameters that I can set, including how the

Web Resource

Adobe Flash — http://adobe.com/products/flash/

Ajax Animator – http://antimatter15.110mb.com/ajaxanimator/build/

SWFTools – http://swftools.org/

SWFMill – http://swfmill.org/

animation should be looped, transitions between images, and others. I finally save all of the pictures as a single GIF formatted file that will display the animation. You can also produce GIF animations using Photoshop Elements, discussed previously.

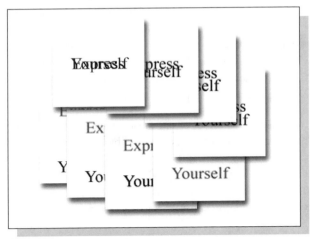

Figure 4.9: GIF Animation

Video Animation

Many video editing programs (including MovieMaker and iMovie, which come preinstalled on Windows and Mac OS computers) have the ability to import still images and then display them for a prescribed amount of time. The result of importing and playing images with gradually changing elements is animation, and it is a quite accessible form for schools with basic video editing software.

One of the classic examples of student-produced video is a project called *The Bernoulli Principle*, produced by students at Palmer Junior Middle School.

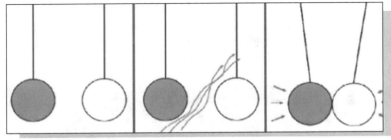

Figure 4.10: Bernoulli

Web Resource

GifBuilder – http://mac.org/graphics/gifbuilder/

This video featured five students illustrating a variety of experiments that demonstrate laws of physics that describe how planes fly. Part of the video is a short animation that graphically demonstrates the concept. To produce this animation, the students drew three still images. (See Figure 4.10: Bernoulli)

Then the pictures were imported into the video editing software they were using, Apple's iMovie, and sequenced between two existing video clips recorded by the team. The effect was a very clear explanation of the concept communicated through animation and voice-over.

Another example was produced in 2004 by kindergarten students at Leo Politi Elementary school as part of Project SMARTArt. The video includes crayon drawings by the students, which were scanned into the computer and then imported into video editing software for sequencing. You can view this award winning student production by going to The Center for Media Literacy site and clicking the Playing with Guns link. The video requires RealMedia to play.

Presentations as Animation

A final type of animation, and perhaps the most accessible to students and teachers, is presentation software. Usually not thought of as animation software, presentation tools, such as Microsoft PowerPoint, Apple's Keynote, or OpenOffice Present, are used routinely by teachers to present content as a more expressive alternative to the chalkboard. The products are powerful communication tools that help us pitch our ideas by utilizing text, imagery, sound, and motion. They help us to hit many different senses and styles of learning.

Using PowerPoint as an instructional tool is often criticized. But if it is taught to students as a communication tool, and their evaluation is based on the quality of their content and effectiveness of their communication, and not on their technical prowess, then these programs should be an essential part of what and how we teach.

One example might be to portray the water cycle. (See Figure 4.11: Water

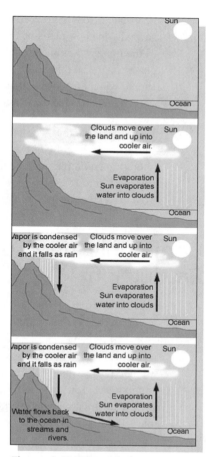

Figure 4.11: Water Cycle

Cycle) We start with a picture of mountains that lead down to the ocean. To build the concept of hydrology, we add to that picture elements that indicate the evaporation of water from the ocean into the air as vapor. Carrying the process through to its next step, we add elements that illustrate how water vapor moves over the mountains and climbs into cooler air where it condenses back into liquid water and falls as rain. Finally, we add a last element indicating how water returns to the ocean through rivers and streams, completing the cycle.

PowerPoint and other presentation programs offer a wide range of transitions that can be employed to move from one slide to another. The tendency among students and teachers is to spend a great deal of time picking the right transition. This is good, as long as this time is invested in selecting the transition that helps communicate the message. For example, one of the popular transitions is Push. This involves the new slide pushing the preceding one off to the right or left. This transition implies a new slide, a new topic, or a new intellectual concept to consider. This would be wrong for our water cycle images, because each slide builds on the previous. A more appropriate transition might be Wipe, which smoothly wipes the new slide across the preceding one. The effect is of the first slide becoming the second—the new element appearing over the original picture. Because the basics of the images (mountains and ocean) are the same, the only thing that would change is the addition of a new image element—clouds. The first slide transitions should wipe left, since that is the direction of the cycle. The later slides should wipe right, since the cycle has looped around to return to the ocean.

Every decision that we make about what we communicate and how we communicate it should be based on what we want to convey and what effect it should have on the audience. As already stated in this chapter, this implies a different kind of assignment that gives the student a topic, an instructional goal, and an authentic audience and how you want to affect that audience.

Communicating Compellingly—Video Production

Of the information that we used during the last century, the medium that was most revered for its technique, technology, and entertainment value was video. Some of us remember and probably still identify video production with huge cameras on rolling tripods, or extensible conveyor arms, operated by highly trained professionals, wired directly into a command booth. We also see a small glassed-in room with an expansive array of controls and video monitors, with which technicians work wizardry on the images that we enjoyed. Over the past decade, video production has become rapidly more accessible to consumers, while the software continued to be highly sophisticated requiring the most state-of-the-art computer systems.

It all started to change in 1999 when Apple Computer introduced iMovie, a dramatically scaled down video editing program that was designed for ease-of-use rather than extensive visual effects. With iMovie, you could connect your digital video camera to your computer, load the video into the software, and edit it with transitions, basic effects, and titles in minutes—the first time you used it. A similar process would have taken hours or days with the previously prevailing desktop video editing software.

We know and accept that video is a powerful communicator. It teaches us by showing how the real world behaves not only across distance, but also across time. It is a means of multidimensional communication, and this is compelling. That we can achieve this style of communication with a $100 video camera and software that comes preinstalled on our computers changes things.

Video is a form of communication that has laid a cultural backbone for generations of viewers. For some of us, the first TVs appeared during our earliest years. Being limited to one channel was common and it often displayed a test pattern.

Through the lens of this device, we grew up seeing people, places, and events that we would never see nor visit in real life. We saw our own planet from outer space, men walking on the moon, dramatic portrayals of historic events, a nation in turmoil over war, and the sanctioned mistreatment of our own citizens. We received a view of the world that had never been available to its inhabitants before and it affected us profoundly.

For some of us, the birth of our children coincided with our first VCR. This new technology gave us control over our video viewing that our parents would not have imagined in the early '50s. What we viewed and when we viewed it was our choice. Today, our children are producing their own video programming, and broadcasting it to global audiences, sometimes with technology they can carry in their pockets.

In a time when TV viewership is down, more people are tuning into online video sharing sites like YouTube. According to a May 2007 Associated Press article, "More than 2.5 million fewer people were watching ABC, CBS, NBC and Fox than at the same time last year, statistics show" (Bauder). In February of that year, informiTV summed up a recent Harris survey, reporting that four in 10 American adults had viewed at least one video on YouTube and that a full third of frequent users of the video sharing site reported that they were watching less TV as a result ("Broadband Meets Broadcast").

Web Resource

informitv – http://informitv.com/articles/2007/02/04/youtubeviewerswatch/

There are several examples of communities who have used their newly found capacity to express ideas with video. One of the first was a project of the political action organization, MoveOn. In their unsuccessful efforts to prevent George Bush from earning a second term, they invited their members to produce 30 second TV ads, produced with consumer video equipment and software. The project was called Bush in 30 Seconds, and the organization received dozens of entries. The winning video was aired on network TV, paid for by MoveOn.

Another, more successful effort occurred in Lafayette, Louisiana, where citizens who wanted true broadband Internet access in their town set about to build their own fiber network. Their telephone and cable companies, Bellsouth and Cox, lobbied the state's legislature to block the project on the grounds of unfair competition. The legislature finally turned the matter back over to the residents for a vote, and the telephone and cable companies invested in professionally produced advertising, making a case against community-run information utilities. Pro-fiber members of the town held a contest to create homemade commercials making a case for competitive broadband Internet, and they won the vote ("Community Connections").

Teaching students to use video will require some shifts in how we, who grew up in the 20th century, view the technology. Once again, our tendency is to integrate video cameras and editing software into the school by producing a daily school news program from inside of a fashioned studio with news anchors, a director, camera people, and console technicians. This is not a bad way to use the technology, especially if all students are cycled through to benefit from all aspects of the production, and as long as instructional objectives are a part of the process.

The problem with this application is that it is highly formatted. Each program will have the same or similar opening, broadcast sections (announcements, sports, in the news, weather), closing, and technical considerations for tying the production together. Because video production has become so cheap and easy to do, the ways that we use it will change, and we need to expand our notions about video to become more of a personal means of communication (multicast) rather than thinking of it only in terms of institutional publishing (broadcast).

Think about how you are currently asking students to demonstrate what they have learned, believe, and know, and imagine how they might express

Web Resources

MoveOn – http://moveon.org/
Bush in 30 Seconds – http://bushin30seconds.org

those ideas using video. A good way to do this is to watch documentaries on The Learning Channel, PBS, The History Channel, or other educational networks. The programs are essentially video research papers that overlay video on top of the words. Watch a documentary one evening, and as you are watching it, write down the ways that it is similar to the writing assignments you give your students and the ways that it is different. Think about asking your students to produce a video essay, or at least to think about how they would communicate the content in their written report if they had access to video recording and editing technology.

Once again, it all comes down to the assignment. If we merely ask students to report what they have learned, then they will learn little more than what is reportable. If we ask them to convince us of an idea, to affect our behavior in some way, then they will learn to use that knowledge. If we can give them the power to deliver a compelling message, then they become owners of that knowledge.

A popular model for helping students to practice skills in employing images and video is Digital Storytelling. There are many projects on the Internet that are labeled as Digital Storytelling, but its original intent was for the artist to compile media that tell a personal story. David Jakes, a national authority, says that Digital Storytelling ". . .merges a personal story with video, still-frame imagery, music, and voice to create a personal multimedia story" (n.d.).

One of the most important parts of the process, according to Jakes, is the final step, removing content. After the story is written and the images selected, what is sometimes the most difficult, and also the most potent task, is to review the material and remove all of the words, sentences, and images that do not contribute directly and clearly to the message of the story. This, Jakes says, always makes it a better story.

The Center for Digital Storytelling houses an archive of digital stories created by teachers who have been through their workshops. You also can see examples of student-produced stories at IslandMovie, a digital storytelling contest open to all Hawaii public school students. A final and rich resource is Stories for Change, an online meeting place for community digital storytelling facilitators and advocates.

Web Resources

Digital Story Telling – http://digitalstorytelling.org/
Center for Digital Story Telling – http://storycenter.org/ to page

Some schools publish teacher and student video productions on YouTube. But to address concerns about the inappropriate content that may be available over the global video sharing site, and to provide a similar tool with a more education specific focus, TeacherTube launched a near YouTube look alike that encourages educators to upload a wide variety of video productions. In their about page, the company urges educators to:

- Upload, tag, and share videos worldwide.

- Upload Support Files to attach your educational Activities, Assessments, Lesson Plans, Notes, and Other file formats to your video.

- Browse hundreds of videos uploaded by community members.

- Find, join, and create video groups to connect with people who have similar interests.

- Customize the experience by subscribing to member videos, saving favorites, and creating playlists.

- Integrate TeacherTube videos on Web sites using video embeds or APIs.

- Make videos public or private—users can elect to broadcast their videos publicly or share them privately with those they invite ("About Us").

Communicating Compellingly—Web Publishing

Web pages are not a new format as much as they are a new place, and this new place carries with it some unique characteristics and opportunities that must be understood in order to fully leverage this new communication medium. One of the unique qualities of Web publishing is its immediacy. When you create or edit the content or layout of your information, and upload the page to the Web server, both the publishing and distribution happen instantly. It is immediately available to your information customers as if it suddenly appeared on their desks. Information publishing becomes more of a conversation because of this immediacy.

This immediacy not only helps to keep your information customers up to date, but it also instills a sense of conversation, that each time the visitor reads your updated pages, they are seeing a current representation of your school, classroom, or personal learning. This sense of conversation brings your information customers back.

Web Resources

islandMovie – http://islandmovie.k12.hi.us/
YouTube – http://youtube.com/

Some Technical Aspects

As mentioned earlier in this book, the technical aspects of publishing information on the Web are minor compared to the challenges of successfully communicating a message. But understanding those technical aspects is critical to fully commanding the medium. Even though few people still build Web pages with HTML (HyperText Markup Language), we will increasingly have opportunities to publish information on the Internet by merely typing our ideas into a Web form and clicking a submit button. Frequently called *content management systems*, many Web sites today are maintained in this way. They edit the content in a Web form and then submit it for update (See Figure 4.12: Content Management). The advantage of content management systems is speed and accessibility. Virtually anyone in your organization can publish his information to the Web site, any time and from any Internet connected computer.

This type of publishing, by filling in the blank, is entirely what blogging is about. Blogging engines are specialized content management systems, and even commenting on blogs you have read gives us an opportunity to better express our responses with formatting. So learning a little HTML is important.

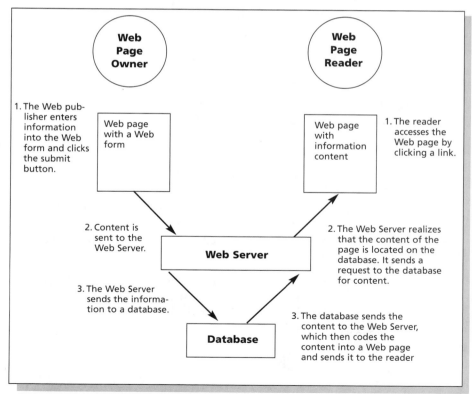

Figure 4.12: Content Management

When entering Web content into a Web form, all that goes through are the words, and we have already explored how formatting (bold, italics, indention, and bullets) can cause information to communicate itself more effectively. Knowing a little bit of HTML, the language of the World Wide Web, can help us to overcome this limitation. If you can insert bolding, italics, or indention codes in with the ideas you type into the form, then you can increase the value of the information by making it easier to read and understand.

Figure 4.13 illustrates a number of HTML codes that help us to compellingly express ideas. They are codes that every teacher should know.

You can practice your HTML coding using an interactive Web form on the page for this chapter at the Web site of this book.

Facilitating School or Classroom Web Sites

Most schools today have their own Web site. Many teachers, as well, publish their own Web presence using a variety of tools, from the very basic to the sophisticated—from School Notes to writing their own pages with raw HTML code. There are a variety of commercial Web publishing systems designed for schools. Among them are:

- School Notes—http://schoolnotes.com/
- TeacherWeb—http://teacherweb.com/
- Think.com—http://think.com/
- My School Online—http://myschoolonline.com/
- eChalk—http://echalk.com/
- ClassWebs—http://classwebs.net/

Some school districts are establishing their own content management systems by utilizing one of the open source projects, such as Drupal. The software can be downloaded, for free, from the Drupal Web site and installed on most standard Web servers. The Drupal site can be configured in a wide variety of ways, and themes can be installed and customized to brand the site for your school or district organization.

Web Resources

Book Web Site – http://davidwarlick.com/redefining_literacy

School Notes – http://schoolnotes.com/

Drupal – http://drupal.org/

Wordpress – http://wordpress.org/

HTML All Teachers Should Know

Basics	- All HTML codes (called tags) are enclosed inside of angle brackets – <tag>. - Most tags consist only of the tag inside of angle brackets – <tag>. - Beginning tags consist only of the tag inside of angle brackets – <tag>. - Ending tags are preceded by a forward slash (/) all inside of angle brackets – </tag>. - HTML tags can be either upper or lower case.
Bold Text	The bold tag is the letter "<B>". When the bold tag is placed in your text, the following letters will be bolded in the Web page. Bolding will end where the ending bold tag is placed. ```Here is some <b>bold</b> text!```
Italics	The italics tag is the letter <i>. When the italics tag is placed in your text, the following letters will be italicized in the Web page. Italics will end where the ending bold tag is placed. ```Here is some <i>italic</i> text!```
Line Breaks	There are two ways to produce a line break. Placing the break tag " " at the end of an intended line will force the following text to the next line. Placing a paragraph tag "<p>" at the end of an intended paragraph will force the following text to the next line skipping a line, creating some white space between the paragraphs.
Indent	There are two ways to indent text. The blockquote tag will indent text at both the left and right margins. Simply place the "</blockquote>" tag at the beginning of a paragraph and the ending "</blockquote>" tag at the end of the paragraph. The second way to indent text is to use the directory tag. This will indent text at only the left margin. Simply place the "<dir>" tag at the beginning of a paragraph and the ending "</dir>" tag at the end of the paragraph.
Bulleted List	The bulleted list is slightly more complicated. First you have to mark the list with the "<ul>" or Unordered List tag. Place the beginning tag "<ul>" at the top of the list and the ending tag "</ul>" at the bottom of the list. Then mark each list item with the "<li>" or List item tag. Place the beginning "<li>" tag at the beginning of each item, and the ending tag ?</li>" at the end of each item. ```Here are my favorite colors <ul> <li>Blue,</li> <li>Red,</li> <li>Yellow, and</li> <li>Green</li> </ul>```
Hyperlink	The heart of the World Wide Web is our ability to connect documents together. To create a hyperlink within your text, place the anchor or "<a>" tag in front of the clickable text and the ending anchor or "</a>" tag at the end. They you must add some additional information to the beginning tag, an *attribute*. After the beginning tag, add a space and href= and the URL of the page you wish to link to. ```They <a href=http://www.loc.gov>library of Congress</a> has information that may be useful to you.```

Figure 4.13: HTML for Teachers

Some schools have even installed Wordpress (a blogging application) and used it for a school Web site. The celebrated Mabry Middle School runs its Web site using Wordpress. They can add more static pages to their site as easily as they can add a blog post. I use Wordpress to run my professional Web site. There are fairly static pages that include a welcome page, a bio page, and pages for each of the keynote and general topic presentations that I deliver at conferences. I use the blog to post online handouts for the individual events at which I present.

What is important about using content management systems, such as Drupal or Wordpress, is that the technology becomes relatively transparent, at least relative to the sophisticated knowledge and skills that were once required. When the technology is less of an issue, then our focus can be applied more to the quality of the communication, or **expressing our ideas compellingly**.

Planning

Regardless of whether you or your students are writing a blog article or creating a classroom or school Web site, the most critical factor for producing a successful online document is planning. Planning can be done by an individual or team, and it entails four steps:

What do you want to accomplish with the Web site? What are your goals? It is critical that you plan for your goals by listing those things that your information customers can do to help you accomplish your goals. Write a list of those actions and behaviors that will help you do your job.

What information should you publish to accomplish your goals? Think, again, of your information customers and their desired behaviors. You need to identify information that will provoke those behaviors and assist them in accomplishing them.

How should your information appear on the screen? Information design is probably the most difficult part of building a Web site. We have already listed some of the ways that text can be formatted to communicate itself more effectively. Also consider if information will communicate itself better as a picture, graph, chart, table, sound, or video. It is about communication.

Implement your plan, evaluate for success, and adapt. I want to add one note about creating a classroom or school Web site. If you do not have one, make one, and use the planning process above to accomplish it. Building a Web page is not difficult, especially if your district can employ a content management system to support teacher Web publishing. Your classroom Web site is a window on your classroom. It reveals what and how you are teaching, and how well your students are learning. Frankly, Web publishing can more effectively serve as an accountability method than annual standardized tests. Your students' parents and your community want pictures, ideas, stories, and they want to see results more than they want to see statistics.

Finally, a classroom or school Web site will help you do your job, if you plan. If you want to see students take greater care with their homework assignments, post assignment details and policies on your site. If you want to involve parents in special projects, but limit how they are to contribute, publish the project details and specify how parents and other caregivers can support the students in their work. If you want to improve the efficiency of getting students off the campus and on their way home after school, then publish a map of the parking and pickup areas with clear instructions on how parents should pick up their children, and format the page so that it can be printed and carried in the door pocket of a car. Web publishing solves problems and accomplishes goals, when we plan with these ends in mind.

Programming as a Communication Skill

Let us examine one more type of communication—talking to your computer in its language. Certainly, the goal is not to make everyone a programmer. Most of us do not have the temperament to sit and write computer code all day. But there are three important reasons why we and our students should have some experience in programming computers.

First of all, learning to program a computer helps to demystify the tool. Computers can appear to be almost magical to us. However, their wizardry comes from highly complex arrangements of very simple instructions: add, subtract, listen, remember, and display. If students have some experience in commanding their computers at this basic level, they will see the machine for what it is—a tool.

The second reason that students should have some experience with programming is that some of them may decide, based on the experience, to become programmers in the future. Part of the power of the computer is the fact that we can transform it into many different things by the instructions we give it, and if we can instruct the machine, we can shape it into tools that help us on a personal level.

Web Resource

Computer Research Association – http://cra.org/

Finally, programming computers almost always involves higher order thinking. MIT's Seymour Papert and many others have written extensively about programming as a means for instilling strategic thinking skills, especially through his landmark book, *Mindstorms*.

We also need more programmers. Patrick Thibodeau, in a March 2008 story in *ComputerWorld*, reported on recent Computing Research Association findings that the number of students graduating in computer science studies has significantly declined since 2004. The report indicates that 14,185 students graduated with CS degrees in the 2003-2004 school year. By contrast, for the 2006-07 academic year, only 8,021 graduated.

Opportunities for Students to Program Computers

There have been many attempts to make programming computers accessible to mere mortals. The earliest personal computers required programming, because there was almost no commercial software available. This is probably the only reason why I am programming today, because I had to teach myself how to program my Radio Shack computer.

One example of accessible programming was Apple Computer's HyperCard (1987) (Wikipedia contributors, "HyperCard"). Designed to allow anyone to create small applications to perform specific tasks, HyperCard gave thousands of people the ability to shape their computers for their needs. Much could be done simply by pulling down menus, adding buttons, and describing what should happen as a result of clicking those buttons. There was a simple, yet powerful programming language associated with HyperCard called *HyperTalk*. With HyperTalk, a Mac user could create small but sophisticated personal applications. Since the early Internet was almost exclusively associated with UNIX and Macintosh computers, the earliest HTML editors were personal HyperCard tools created by their users. Seymour Papert's *Mindstorms* described a programming language developed at MIT that enabled elementary children to program their computers, creating a pet turtle that could be directed to draw simple and intricate shapes and designs on the computer screen. Dr. Gary Stager, a proponent of teaching children to program and a colleague of Papert's, hosts a rich resource page for educators who are interested in using Logo and Microworlds, a larger Logo environment.

> **Web Resources**
>
> Microworlds – http://microworlds.com/
> Learning With Logo - http://stager.org/logo.html
> Lifelong Kindergarten Group – http://llk.media.mit.edu/

One promising avenue for drawing more students into an interest in programming is video games. The Lifelong Kindergarten Group at MIT has developed an object oriented programming language, enabling youngsters to develop basic video games and multimedia presentations. Called *Scratch*, the language utilizes graphical tools that are dragged into a work area and assembled. In a sense, the programming is building a machine that controls objects on the screen, causing them to interact with each other.

So, is this literacy? If we limit our notions of literacy to the ability to read and write text on paper, then programming is something entirely different. However, if we define literacy as those skills involved in using information to accomplish goals, and that information is increasingly digital and computers are becoming the prevailing tool for using information, then there may well be a perspective that would call programming a basic literacy skill.

> " ... if we define literacy as those skills involved in using information to accomplish goals, and that information is increasingly digital and computers are becoming the prevailing tool for using information, then there may well be a perspective that would call programming a basic literacy skill. "

Regardless, we know that children are perfectly capable of learning basic programming and, often, more sophisticated techniques.

Conclusion

Earlier in this book, you learned of a new world Internet speed record. Internet2 technicians successfully sent 9 gigabytes of data 20,000 miles in one second. To put this into perspective, 9 gigabytes is the equivalent of more than 250 sets of encyclopedias. Now just imagine what you could do with 250 sets of encyclopedias being streamed into your computers every second. If you cannot think of much, then the point is made. Who can handle that much text that fast? Who would want to?

However, when we think about 9 gigabytes in terms of high definition video, then possibilities begin to emerge: motion pictures, multimedia manuals, virtual field trips, fully interactive textbooks—all on demand. The point is that we are not producing this amazing capacity to communicate in order to send e-mail. We are producing this capacity to communicate because we know

Web Resource

Scratch – http://scratch.mit.edu/

that in the 21st century we are going to communicate with multimedia, and it will be our students who are filling this capacity. So it is essential that at the same time that we teach them to write, we also teach them to communicate with images, animation, sound, and video.

Action Items

Directors of Technology

- Rewrite your district's acceptable use policy (AUP) to address the expectation that students and teachers will communicate with emerging digital network technologies, taking advantage of new opportunities to teach, learn, and manage education by engaging in conversations online. Also address safety issues related to Internet communication.

- Consider establishing a district wide content management system (CMS) that enables professional staff to run and maintain their own virtual classroom presences (classroom Web sites).

- Establish a district Web site that is designed to showcase student (and teacher) products on an ongoing basis. Provide opportunities for the public to comment on the work (via Web forms) and post appropriate comments along with the productions.

- Explore, plan, and implement venues for teachers to display student-produced information products. Collaborate with the local public library, community college, banks, coffee shops, and other places to display student productions.

- Consider establishing RSS feeds for student produced media so that interested members of the community can subscribe to and receive these artifacts of learning throughout the year.

- Offer staff development opportunities for teachers and students on computer graphics, Web design, information architecture, music composition, video production, and creative writing. Be careful that the focus is always compelling communication rather than the technology.

- Facilitate on-demand support for school principals, tech facilitators, media specialists, and teachers in planning for integrating computer-assisted production in their instructional process.

- Work to provide appropriate hardware and software in sufficient quantity so that teachers can conveniently implement their plans.

- Work toward placing graphic software on every computer, digital still and video cameras in every classroom, and numerous music composition stations in every school.

Principals and Head Teachers

- Understand that the accountability that parents and the community truly want to see is what teachers are teaching, how they are teaching it, what students are learning, and how well they are learning it. Look for opportunities to showcase exemplary examples of each to your community, and leverage those opportunities to help you accomplish your goals.

- Plan a school Web site and a way for all teachers and other professional staff members to publish information to that site. Require that all teachers have a classroom Web site and demonstrate how their Web site helps them do their job. Include in your expectations and your teachers' evaluations the ways that they are using digital communication to accomplish their goals.

- Think of your school as more than its building. Include in your vision of the school all of the information products (text, images, songs, video) that are produced by students and teachers. Help the community to include these products in their vision of the school.

- Work with the media specialist, tech facilitator, teachers, and central office staff to plan for wise and sufficient procurement of hardware and software. Expect information production to become a part of every learning environment in your schools.

- Invite community comments on student and teacher work.

- Establish a media production team at your school and assign them with the responsibility of recording the significant events and nuanced qualities of the school year. Have both upper- and underclassmen on the team so that experienced students train less experienced students. Assign supervision to the media specialist and tech facilitator.

Media Specialists

- Assist the principal in planning and implementing the school's Web site.

- Include in your media center Web site a section that showcases student productions.

- Establish displays in the media center (and beyond) for showcasing student productions.

- Establish an archive of student productions, both digital and non-digital, and catalog them so that students and teachers have access to their work. Include with each product all of its authors and their specific contributions. Make these products available to future students for improvement.

- Work with the tech facilitator (or music teacher) to establish a music production station in the media center. As student teams produce musical selections, archive and catalog them with other students' productions.

- Work with the tech facilitator to form media production clubs in your school for still photography, video production, music production, animation, and more.

- Think of your library media center as a *Kinko's for Kids*. Build it out and advertise it as a place where students and teachers can come, not only to find and consume content, but also as a place where they can produce original content.

School Tech Facilitators

- Assist the principal and media specialist in planning and implementing the school's Web site.

- Establish a music production station in the media center, and train selected students to use the hardware and software. Help them form a team to serve as consultants to other students and teachers in producing music for their presentations and other information products. (If the school has a music teacher, this function should be performed by that person.)

- Assist the principal and media specialist in procurement of production hardware and software by compiling an ongoing folder of specifications and reviews (formal and casual) of various media production equipment and software.

- Establish an inventory of hardware and software and implement a check-out plan that makes it easy for teachers to acquire additional equipment when needed. Make sure that all teachers have access to cameras in their classrooms at all times, software for downloading images from the cameras, and training to operate the cameras and software.

- Encourage the teachers in your school to blog about their media experiments, successes, and failures, and subscribe to those blogs. Encourage other teachers to subscribe to each other's blogs.

- Work with the media specialist to form media production clubs in your school for still photography, video production, music production, and animation.

- Work with media specialists to outfit their center as a content production workshop.

Teachers

- Have at least one digital still camera in your classroom, charged, and at your disposal at all times.

- Have a digital video camera in your classroom, charged, and at your disposal at all times. Be ready at any time to take videos of events that might be useful in the future. Think of it as a note-taking tool.

- When going on a field trip, have numerous digital still and video cameras available to students for recording important aspects of the trip.

- Allow students to select information products that were constructed by past students and improve on their work as a way of completing assignments.

- Coordinate with the media specialists on the creation of a library of student productions.

- Identify students with a particular interest in music, and connect them with a media specialist or tech facilitator for training on music compositions.

Students

- As you watch movies, TV programs, documentaries, or listen to music, ask yourself these questions:
    - In what ways did this performance affect what I know and believe?
    - How did the performance accomplish this effect?
    - In what ways did this performance affect me emotionally?
    - How did the performance accomplish this effect?
    - What visual or auditory effects did the director or producer employ that were especially effective.

- Join clubs related to media production (video, photography, graphic, text, music).

- As you are learning to use production hardware and software, imagine how the equipment or software might be improved in ways that your teachers are not explaining. Imagine how the equipment and software may be used in the future to make the process easier or more powerful.

- When you know that programs will be occurring on TV or in the movie theatre that are related in some way to your classroom studies, tell your teachers and ask if you can get extra credit for viewing them and then reporting on what you learned.

- If you are especially interested in video production, art, music composition, or photography, work toward acquiring your own equipment and software, and develop your skills. Have fun doing it.

Parents

- Visit your school's Web site regularly. If you do not see examples of student and teacher productions, ask that they be made available for viewing.

- If you find student and teacher information productions on the school's Web site, and if there is an opportunity, make productive comments about the works.

- If you have some knowledge, skill, or experience in media production of any type, volunteer your time at the school to help students and teachers learn from your expertise.

- If your children express a special interest in video production, art, music composition, or photography, help them acquire their own equipment and software, and develop your skills as well.

- If you do not have one already, purchase a digital still or video camera and begin a library of family events.

CHAPTER 5

Ethics and Context

W e find ourselves working and playing within a new information environment. It has natural laws and tendencies. It is, in a sense, an ecosystem with interplay and dependency. It operates well under some conditions and not so well under others. In the same fashion that natural environments can be threatened by counter-ecological actions, our information environment is equally fragile. We have existed and prospered within information environments for many years, and our definitions of literacy have described skills necessary to work that information environment to accomplish our goals.

Ethics and the Age of Information

For the purposes of this book, *literacy* is described as the skills involved in using information to accomplish goals. But literacy also should describe behaviors related to how we leverage our information environment to accomplish goals. Historically, as people and communities became socially and economically inter-connected and dependent on each other, margins of behavior emerged that promoted the amiable and productive use of property. They defined acts that were detrimental to people and their communities. For instance, if one farmer stole crops from another or ranchers dammed up a river that irrigated farmland, it had a direct and negative impact on the people, families, and communities who depended on the land for their sustenance and prosperity. As another example, if an agricultural community planted the same crops year after year without attention to replenishing the nutrients in the soil, it ultimately had a devastating effect on the well being of all of its members.

Making appropriate use of natural resources could be characterized as a corridor through which responsible behaviors were practiced for the good of all. On either side of these corridors were behaviors that were harmful to other people or wasted resources and opportunities. Likewise, there is a corridor of responsible behavior with regard to information, along with margins of inappropriate, wasteful, and dangerous behaviors. Drawing the line between these actions continues to be a challenge, but it is critical that conversations about and descriptions of these behaviors be a part of what we consider the basic literacy skills that our children should learn.

Information as Property

Consider the story of Christine Pelton, a former biology teacher in Piper, Kansas. It is a story that you may already be aware of, but it bears repeating within the context of defined corridors of behavior. Ms. Pelton had a rule in her classroom. If students plagiarized in their work, they received a zero. This was a hard rule, and students and parents signed contracts acknowledging this rule.

The last assignment that Ms. Pelton made was called the "Leaf Project," requiring students to collect leaves from 20 local trees and write a report for each. When the reports were turned in, and Ms. Pelton started to review them, she found that many of the papers included identical sentences and that some of the writing was not consistent with the normal writing levels of her students. She took the reports to **TurnItIn.com**, an online plagiarism detection service, and found evidence that 28 of the students had plagiarized information from the Internet in their reports. These students received failing grades for their work.

The principal of the school supported Ms. Pelton in her grading. However, under pressure from the students' parents, the school board ruled that the students should receive a failing grade only for the research part of the assignment (about 40 percent of the grade) and that the weighting of the project be reduced so that the students would pass for the semester. The day after the ruling, Christine Pelton resigned. Before the beginning of the next school year, her principal also resigned along with 30 percent of the district's other teachers and counselors, because the story, which went national, devastated the

Web Resource

Turnitin – http://turnitin.com/

community's reputation. The superintendent eventually resigned under a settlement agreement (Wilgoren).

What played out in Piper, Kansas, was an inevitable clash between an older 20th century belief system toward information and a newer 21st century information environment. The pivotal point is that sometime between the time that the parents and school board members attended school and the educational environment promoted by Christine Pelton, the value of information changed. During the 1950s and '60s, when I was in school, the information economy was based on a medieval structure. The producers and distributors of information were a restrictive nobility of powerful publishers and broadcast networks that produced and distributed information to the rest of us, the vast information consumers—the serfs. This relationship between a few information producers and a multitude of consumers was out of balance, from our perspective, especially as information was already beginning to play a crucial role in our lives. As information users, we felt victimized by price-fixing, editorializing, commercial interests, and a catering to the lowest common denominator of consumer interests.

This imbalance of power between information producers and consumers instilled in us, the consumers, a perceived right to do with information what we wanted. We were taught not to copy text from the encyclopedia, but if we exercised the semantics of paraphrasing, then it was okay to use the information of others. We were taught to create a bibliography, but not why. I graduated from high school believing that the only place you cited your sources of information was in research papers. I was also fairly sure that I would be writing my last research paper sometime shortly before I graduated from college. So citing information sources seemed to be an exclusively academic exercise and not part of the real world of work and life.

Information is changing, not only in where you find it and what it looks like, but also where it comes from. An increasingly accessible Web, especially in light of recently emerging applications like blogging, podcasting, and sites like Flickr and YouTube, mean that many of us, if not most of us, our students included, are information producers and intellectual property owners. Self-publishing services like Lulu, Aventine Press, and CreateSpace have enabled thousands of authors to publish and market books, people who would not have been able to penetrate the traditional publishing world.

My Web site receives more than a half-million page views a day from nearly 100 countries. These are people who are accessing information and information services that are produced and

Web Resources

Lulu – http://lulu.com/
Aventine Press – http://aventinepress.com/
CreateSpace - http://createspace.com/

distributed by one person from a small office in the basement of his home. The fact that each of us can publish information and distribute it to a global audience dramatically changes the balance between producer and consumer. "We the Media," a phrase probably coined by reporter, author, and blogger, Dan Gilmore, is used extensively to describe a new information environment that distinguishes between information consumer and information producer by what you are doing at the moment, rather than who you are. And so, when the information that we consider using may have been produced, at great effort, by another teacher, student, neighbor, or family member, we may tend to consider the ownership of that information in a different way than we did in a feudal environment. Few of us would cheat a neighbor in the same way we may be willing to cheat a large multinational broadcast corporation.

Christine Pelton understood this and insisted that her students respect information as valuable property that was owned by somebody else. The parents who appealed to the board of education to change Ms. Pelton's grading policy treated information as an abundant commodity whose ownership and credit is less important than its availability. Neither is at fault. It is a sign of the rapidly changing nature of information.

> **The best way to help students understand and appreciate information as valuable property is to make them property owners.**

The best way to help students understand and appreciate information as valuable property is to make them property owners. As a result of **The Digital Millennium Copyright Act of 1998**, all information is assumed to be copyrighted unless specifically labeled otherwise. All formal documents, informal notes, e-mails, and student works are automatically copyrighted. To use information created by someone else requires permission either granted as a courtesy or purchased. Documents are not required to display the ubiquitous copyright message in order to be considered copyrighted, although they may still be included.

Placing this designation does, however, convey a sense of property and importance to a document, and imply ownership. So, when students are asked to produce an information product, whether it is a poem, report, Web page, multimedia presentation, work of art, or original story, they might also be asked to label their ownership of the document by placing the copyright text at the bottom of their pages.

Copyright © 2008 by *student name*

We should also develop the habit of talking about students' work as belonging to them. Rather than referring to "this work," we should say, "your paper," "your ideas," "your work," "your research." We should also explicitly ask their permission before using any parts of their work as examples either in class or as part of a student showcase.

Another quality of information products is their infinite expandability. In the working world, information products are rarely created in a vacuum. We are always building on the work of others. We start with this report, adapt that curriculum, update a five-year-old policy, or combine the writings of several experts into a well-crafted persuasive message. This practice of mixing information is almost a *modus operandi* for many of our students, as they mix videos from YouTube, audio from CDs, and other information to create new information products. Stanford University law professor Lawrence Lessig and other copyright activists use the term *remix culture* to describe a society that allows and even encourages derivative works.

One example of this remix practice is *machinima*. We have already explored the concept, but the technique has become so wide spread that *Machinima for Dummies* (Hancock and Ingram) was recently added to the cascade of ". . . for Dummies" books.

Machinima and other media re-mixing practices indicate a major divide between the way that my generation thinks about information and my children's generation. For us, information is a product that we purchase and consume, i.e. a book to be read, a CD to be listened to, a DVD to be watched. For my children's generation, information is a raw material. At least part of the value of the information that they encounter is in what they can do with it—how they can remix it with other content.

This tendency to mix and remix information holds huge potential for learning, as students might be asked to compellingly express what they are learning, within the context of their experience and prior knowledge, by finding content and remixing it into a new, useful, and interesting information product. While the potentials are enormous, the issues of information property are called into play and should be called into the conversations of the classroom. What are the copyright and courtesy considerations of mixing images from Flickr, songs from a favorite CD, and action from a favorite video game?

Courtesy comes first, and the point should be made, understood, and discussed that information is property. Creating media costs its producer time and talent. If it is useful to someone else in helping them accomplish their goal, solve a problem, or entertain themselves, then the information has value. Because it costs and has value, it should be considered a property, to be respected.

Web Resource

Lawrence Lessig's Blog – http://lessig.org/blog/

> " ...the ethical use of information is a literacy skill, a literacy practice. "

It is not the purpose of this book to give legal advice about copyright and fair use. Carol Simpson's *Ethics in School Librarianship* and Doug Johnson's *Learning Right from Wrong in the Digital Age* are excellent sources for information and ideas on this topic. The point that is essential here is that the ethical use of information is a literacy skill, a literacy practice.

To further help students think more positively about their information experiences, a school library might establish a collection of student produced information products that have been completed and evaluated, and then archived for future use. The work that students perform has value to future students and teachers, and the authors will continue to receive credit for their contributions. For example, if a middle school class is studying volcanoes, the teacher might hand a student a printed report that was written and turned in the previous year along with a digital version of the report. As an assignment, she might ask the student to use the content from the report and produce a multimedia presentation that enhances the ideas through images, animation, sound, and video. It becomes an activity of research, organization, and media production. Another student might be given a multimedia presentation and asked to write and attach text that complements the existing media, providing conceptual explanations for the presentation. In each scenario, the student is building on the work of previous students, producing a far more important and powerful work as a result. Each student, past and present, would receive credit appropriate to her contribution. An important function of librarians would be the organization of student work libraries that can be used as assignment starters or as instructional products by teachers.

Creative Commons

Creative Commons (CC) has been mentioned several times already in this book. The organization that drives it was established in 2001 by Stanford law professor Lawrence Lessig. A principal aim of Creative Commons is to expand the range and quantity of media that can legally be built upon and shared. Their Web site states:

> Too often the debate over creative control tends to the extremes. At one pole is a vision of total control—a world in which every last use of a work is regulated and in which "all rights reserved" (and then some) is the norm. At the other end is a vision of anarchy—a world in which creators enjoy a wide range of freedom but are left vulnerable to exploitation. Balance, compromise, and moderation—once the driving forces of a copyright system that valued innovation and protection equally—have become endangered species ("About").

Web Resource

Creative Commons – http://creativecommons.org/

Creative Commons seeks to strike this balance by providing for information producers the ability to fine tune the rights they reserve and the rights they are willing to give to consumers of their content. It is very easy to establish a Creative Commons license for your digital image, text, music, or video. Here is a step-by-step process:

1.   Send your Web browser to http://creativecommons.org/.

2.   Near the top of the page, click **License Your Work**.

3.   You will be presented with a set of options to determine rights that users have of your information. (See Figure 5.1: Creative Commons Form)

choose license

With a Creative Commons license, **you keep your copyright** but allow people to copy and distribute your work provided they give you credit — and only on the conditions you specify here. For those new to Creative Commons licensing, we've prepared a list of things to think about. If you want to offer your work with no conditions, choose the public domain.

Allow commercial uses of your work?
(•) Yes (more info)
( ) No (more info)

Allow modifications of your work?
(•) Yes (more info)
( ) Yes, as long as others share alike (more info)
( ) No (more info)

Jurisdiction of your license (more info)
| United States ▾ |

Click to include more information about your work.

| Select a License |

Figure 5.1: Creative Commons Form

4.   As an example, let's say that you have created a diagram for your science class that effectively illustrates the water cycle, and you are including it on your classroom Web site. You might select the options described in the following steps.

5.   Option one refers to commerce. Are you willing to "Allow commercial uses of your work?" You are probably not agreeable to commercial organizations using your diagram in their textbook or other marketable product. So, you would click "No."

6.   Option two refers to your willingness to allow others to take your diagram and alter it in some way that is useful to them. There are three options here. You can click "Yes" to allow others to modify your diagram. You can click "Yes, as long as others share alike." This means that if someone alters your work and makes it available on the Internet, for example, then they are agreeing to pass on the same rights to anyone else who might want to use and alter their version of your work. Finally, you can click "No," indicating that you are not willing to have others modify your diagram.

7. Finally, you can select the jurisdiction of your license, the country, or government under which you want your Creative Commons license applied most directly. This causes the license to be worded in a way that complies with local copyright laws. I would select, "United States."

8. You can also "Click to include more information about your work." This allows you to include in your license the format of your work (audio, video, image, text, interactive), the title of the work, the name of the producer or author, the work's URL, its source work, and the URL of other permission information.

9. When the submit button is clicked, the work section above is returned where you can select the type of Creative Commons badge you would like to have available on your Web page. (See Figure 5.2: Creative Commons Badge).

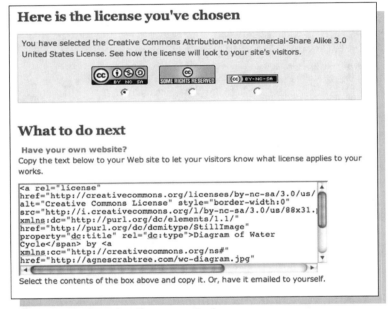

Figure 5.2: Creative Commons Badge

10. When you have clicked the radio button for the desired badge, highlight and copy the code that is produced in the large text area box, and then paste the code into your Web page. The code will cause the select badge to appear in your page, and, when checked, a page will appear that describes the nature of your Creative Commons license and the rights you are extending to information consumers.

Creative Commons was first tested in the courts by podcast godfather, Adam Curry, in 2006. A Dutch tabloid included a photo in one of its stories that Curry had posted on his Flickr page, images that he had specifically licensed under Creative Commons denying commercial use. The Dutch court decided in favor of Curry, and although the tabloid avoided having to pay penalty by not repeating the offense, the decision set a precedent of legal binding with regard to copyright (Jones).

Perhaps, rather than having students flag their works as copyrighted only, it may be more useful to ask them also to license their work under Creative Commons. Not only would it allow their works to be used by other students and teachers, but educating students about Creative Commons license would enable more conversations about information as property, and provoke more thought about the intellectual property of others.

Information Reliability

The value of information comes from its appropriateness in helping you accomplish your goals. It also can be measured by the time, talent, and knowledge that was spent in producing the information. However, the ultimate value is based on its accuracy, validity, and reliability—on its authority. If the content:

- Comes from a recognized or credentialed expert on the topic,

- Logically applies to the task at hand, and

- Can be depended upon to continue to apply to the task at hand,

then its value is increased. As we evaluate our students' information products, a large part of the assessment should be based on the value or potential value of the product. Who is its intended audience? In what ways might it benefit them? How successful were the students or teams of students in accomplishing their goal? And, to what degree have they enhanced the product with authority? If students understand that employing the assistance of expert, logical, and reliable sources in their information products adds to the value of their work, and consequently a more favorable evaluation, then they may be more likely to critically evaluate the sources and properly cite the work of others.

This is one, among many reasons why the assignments we give our students should be authentic, with specific audiences and meaningful goals in mind. Asking students to merely write a report about a topic made sense from a purely instructional viewpoint within information-scarce learning environments. However, it makes little sense to students who are learning how to interact within information-abundant learning environments. In addition, writing basic reports about teacher assigned topics makes it too easy for students to paraphrase large chunks of text or images into their word processors. Even if the students cite the resources, they may not have truly examined the information within the context of the real world or its impacts on life.

Some Authentic Assignments based on Curriculum Standards

Grade Level and Subjects	Standard	Assignment
Grade 3 Healthful Living	The learner will direct personal health behaviors in accordance with own health status and susceptibility to major health risks.	Ask students to develop a poster with a set of rules for personal behavior for a local summer camp to be printed and displayed in camp cabins. Audience: Young campers Goal: Prevent potential health problems
Grade 4 Mathematics	Spatial Sense, Measurement, and Geometry - The learner will demonstrate an understanding and use of the properties and relationships in geometry, and standard units of metric and customary measurement.	Ask teams of students to create a blueprint for the school of the future. Ask them to base their design on interviews with students and teachers. Audience: School planners of the future Goal: Promote schools that are student and teacher centered.
Grade 5 Music	The learner will compose and arrange music within specified guidelines.	Ask students to compose and record an original musical piece to accompany a multimedia presentation they are creating for another subject. Audience: Other students Goals: Depends on the multimedia assignment
Grade 6 Science	Describe ways in which organisms interact with each other and with non-living parts of the environment: ■ Limiting factors ■ Coexistence/Cooperation/ Competition ■ Symbiosis	Select a geographic area that is currently undeveloped. Ask students to research the impact of urban development on the ecosystem, and then project the potential impact of development in the selected area. Audience: Urban planners and voters Goal: Promote development that is less detrimental to the environment
Grade 7 Social Studies	Geography - The learner will locate major physical features and suggest the influence of their location on life in Africa and Asia.	Research the physical features of a country in Africa or Asia and then design and produce a brochure for a tourist company. Audience: Vacationers Goal: Persuade vacationers to visit the assigned country
Grade 9-12 Second Languages	The learner will engage in conversation and exchange information and opinions orally and in writing in the target language.	Establish a relationship with a class in a country that speaks the target language. Agree upon an issue and then require students to send messages in the target language that explain their country's position on the issue. Audience: Students in another country with a different language Goal: Share national perspectives

Figure 5.3: Authentic Assignments

If the student is assigned to create an information product for a specific audience and with a specific goal in mind, and the teacher's evaluation of the product will be at least partly based on the intrinsic value of the work, then the student will need to find information that supports the task, decode and evaluate the information, assemble it in a way that addresses the audience and goal, and publish the information in a medium that will most likely result in success.

The assignments in Figure 5.3 are not new nor are they especially creative. However, they all involve an authentic audience and a meaningful goal for that audience. The authenticity of the assignment forces students to do a very important thing. They must think about information in terms of its accuracy, validity, reliability, and value and make decisions about where, how, and why it will be used. This is a powerful learning condition.

Information Infrastructure

Understanding information as property that is reliably valuable is only two-thirds of the ethics issue. We must also help students to understand that in a society that depends so critically on information as a fabric of its existence, information can be an enormous tool for good and a devastating cause of harm. Consider that in 2002 a handful of corporate executives, in an attempt to deceive stockholders and employees, inadvertently brought the U.S. economy to its knees. Certainly the dot.com meltdown, attack of September 11, and subsequent war in Iraq contributed to the persistently weak economies of 2002 and 2003. But, the deceptive actions of these few very powerful people pulled the foundation out from under the economy, a foundation of trust.

When information becomes the glue that holds together our business and social institutions, that information must be rock-solid reliable, and its reliability is no less critical than the reliability of our roads, bridges, sea ports, airports, and power grid. Our information infrastructure was seriously eroded by the 2002 scandals, caused by greed and a disregard for the truth. During recent decades, professional success has been defined in terms of windfalls, IPOs, corporate culture, multibillion dollar buy outs, and early retirement. These were the measures of success, and succeeding in these terms often outweighed the integrity that clearly characterized previous generations. It is business as *The Art of War*. As one Piper High School student said,

> . . . I would say that in this day and age, cheating is almost not wrong. Because it is any way that you can get an advantage.

These are words spoken by a student of the 1980s and '90s. As we teach students the value of information, it is crucial that we teach the value of what is true. Information is the foundation of our institutions, and that foundation is only as sturdy as it is truthful.

Of equal concern is the uninterrupted and undiluted flow of the information. A recent survey of 2000 U.S. households found that computer viruses, spyware, and phishing cost consumers approximately $7 billion dollars over two years (Claburn). To be fair, a thorough search for statistics on the cost of these abuses will reveal amounts ranging from $10 to $100 billion. Regardless of the particular report, the unethical abuse of our information infrastructure is costing us a lot.

According to a study from Richi Jennings, spam alone cost the world $50 billion in 2005, about $19 billion just in the United States. The report projected that numbers would double in 2007, costing the country $35 billion. To put this into perspective, according to the Copenhagen Consensus, we could bring HIV/AIDS, worldwide, under control for only $27 billion, less than what my country will spend protecting itself from spam (Kerr).

Information is power, and 21st century literacy equips children and adults, learners and teachers with powerful tools. We have at our disposal a global electronic library of information, much of it coming out of our own communities. We are increasingly gaining access to potent digital tools that can access, alter, and communicate that information in infinite and persuasive ways. Consider Nelson Mandela and Slobodan Milosevic. They each led their nations in dramatically new directions by telling compelling new stories. Mandela told a story of reconciliation. Milosevic told a story of hatred and revenge. They brought about change, good and bad, with information.

To make some sense of information ethics, I want to return to one of the shifts in the nature of information that was described earlier in this book. Over the past 15 years we have seen an enormous shift from a purely broadcast society (production and distribution of information by a few) to a multicast society (production and distribution of information by many/all). To explore the ethical responsibilities of information workers, I want to step back to the broadcast model and examine one of the primary sources of content at that time—journalists. It is the job of journalists to collect information about conditions in our social, cultural, economic, and physical environments and report on them in a way that their readers continue to be

Web Resources

Copenhagen Consensus – http://copenhagenconsensus.com/
Society of Professional Journalists – http://spj.org/

The job of a journalist is to expose what is true, employ information, and express ideas compellingly.

informed as democratic citizens. The job of a journalist is to *expose what is true, employ information*, and *express ideas compellingly*.

Perhaps more than any other profession, journalism has practiced, for many years, the levels of literacy described in this book, a contemporary literacy for the 21st century. They seek out information, decode it, evaluate, process, and communicate it in compelling ways. Journalists aspire to high standards of ethics, reflecting the importance of their mission and their responsibility to society. The Society of Professional Journalists (SPJ) has published a Code of Ethics for its members.

I am using, with the permission of their executive director, the SPJ's code of ethics as a springboard to model an information code of ethics for teachers and students. It addresses the ethical issues discussed in this chapter, and does so in a proactive and productive way, making the information producer and user responsible. The major goals of this code of ethics are:

1. To describe a desire to seek and share the truth of any issue, understanding that the truth extends far beyond the mere accuracy of facts.

2. To minimize the harm that may result from the expression of information.

3. To apply accountability to information producers and users for the outcomes of their work.

4. To guard the information infrastructure from physical or digital breakdown.

Goal number one describes a need to pursue what is true. When considering the truth of the information at hand, students and teachers must be able to answer these:

- Is the information accurate to a degree that is consistent with the goal at hand?

- Under what conditions will the information remain accurate?

- Is it accurate from relevant perspectives (Middle Eastern, African, consumer, employee, young, old, others)?

The second goal speaks directly to the intended or inadvertent consequences of information. Compellingly expressed information has the power to affect how people feel, what they believe, the decisions they make, and how they

Web Resources

SPJ's Code of Ethics – http://spj.org/ethics_code.asp

interact with other people. There is enormous potential for improving our condition with information, and equal potential for harm and suffering. This potential must be a part of every decision made with regard to information. Information users must ask these questions:

- Will communicating the information cause harm or threaten harm to any one person or group of people?

- Will communicating this information in a specific format cause harm or threaten to harm any one person or group of people?

- Will not communicating the information cause harm or threaten harm to any one person or group of people?

- In what ways will communicating the information positively impact any one person or group of people?

Another aspect of this goal is respect for other people's intellectual property. Compiling information, processing it, and building a new and valuable information product is hard work. This makes it valuable, at least to the builder, and absolutely essential that credit be given to the owners of all information that is used.

The third goal of our information code of ethics refers to accountability. The journalist holds herself or himself accountable by applying a by-line by their report. They are putting their reputation behind their information product and making themselves available to defend their work. In order to assure the safe use of information, those who access, employ, and express it must be accountable for their actions and the outcomes. This means that any information work must include, as an essential component, the author's willingness to defend the work in terms of its truthfulness and the harm it might cause. All information products should include supporting information or references to supporting information about the content so that consumers can evaluate the quality of the product for themselves.

The final element of an information code of ethics deals with the information infrastructure on which our civilization has come to depend so heavily. This information foundation is only as dependable as the hardware and software of the computers and networks where it resides and flows, and these facilities are vulnerable.

During the final edit of the first edition of this book, we were all reeling from the effects of SoBig, a malicious software worm that was introduced to the Internet and impacted not only those computers that were infected, but also many more people as the code was written to attribute the spread of the virus to e-mail addresses taken randomly from address books. Even though I use a Macintosh, which is immune to most viruses, my mailbox was flooded with e-mails automatically issued by mail-managing software alerting me that I had sent a virus. During this time, I was working in northern Wisconsin where I did not have access to e-mail. My mailbox filled up with SoBig related e-mail, causing messages from clients, colleagues, and associates to bounce back as if I no longer existed. This, of course, could affect my business and my income as an independent consultant. We must set standards of behavior that protect this infrastructure and creatively eliminate the desire in people to cause mayhem in cyberspace.

A Student and Teacher Code of Ethics

Following is a code of ethics for students and teachers. It is adapted out of the COE of the Society of Professional Journalists, with the permission of their executive director. This is intended as a model or starting point for information guidelines for your teachers and students, for your classroom or school.

A Student and Teachers Information Code of Ethics

Seek Truth and Express It

Teachers and students should be honest, fair, and courageous in gathering, interpreting, and expressing information for the benefit of others. They should:

- Test the accuracy of information from all sources and exercise care to avoid inadvertent error.

- Always identify sources. The consumers of your information product must be able to make their own judgment of its value.

- Always question the sources' motives.

- Never distort or misrepresent the content of photos, videos, or other media without explanation of intent and permission from the information's owner. Image enhancement for technical clarity is permissible.

- Tell the story of the human experience boldly, even when it is unpopular to do so.

- Examine your own cultural values and avoid imposing those values on others.

- Avoid stereotyping by race, gender, age, religion, ethnicity, geography, sexual orientation, disability, physical appearance, or social status.

- Give voice to the voiceless; official and unofficial sources of information can be equally valid.

- Distinguish between opinion and fact when expressing ideas. Analysis and commentary should be labeled and not misrepresent fact or context.

Minimize Harm

- Ethical teachers and students treat information sources, subjects, colleagues, and information consumers as human beings deserving of respect.

- Gathering and expressing information should never cause harm or threaten to be harmful to any one person or group of people.

- Recognize that private people in their private pursuits have a greater right to control information about themselves than do others.

- Consider all possible outcomes to the information you express, guarding against potential harm to others.

- Never use information from another person without proper citation and permission.

Be Accountable

- Teachers and students are accountable to their readers, listeners, viewers, and to each other.

- Clarify and explain information and invite dialogue about your conduct as a communicator.

- Encourage the information consumer to voice grievances about your information products.

- Admit mistakes and correct them promptly.

- Expose unethical information practices of others.

Respect Information and its Infrastructure

- Information, in the *Information Age*, is property. Information is the fabric that defines much of what we do from day to day, and this rich and potent fabric is fragile.

- Never undertake any action that has the potential to damage any part of this information infrastructure. These actions include, but are not limited to, illegally hacking into a computer system, launching or distributing viruses or other damaging software, physically damaging or altering hardware or software, or publishing information that you know is untrue and potentially harmful.

- Report to proper authorities any activities that could potentially result in harm to the information infrastructure.

- A downloadable MSWord version of this code of ethics is available for downloading from this book's Web site.

Web Resources

Book's Web Site – http://davidwarlick.com/redefining_literacy/

There are two terms that are used numerous times in the code of ethics above, and both have been used in other places in the book. Both terms have been used in other publications and discussions, but they do bear further explanation within the context of this book. They are *Information Product* and *Information Consumer*. Both terms owe their phrasing to the notion that information will be the raw material with which people will work during the Information Age, and with this information raw material, we will construct a wide variety of *information products*, which people will consume—*information consumers*.

During the 20th century, we could talk about students' writings, or art, or posters. However, today we may refer to a much wider and richer array of products when describing their work. It may be writing or art. However, the work may manifest itself as a Web page, or multimedia production using presentation software. It may be a virtual reality experience, a performance, or a piece of software. Each of these is a product that, when constructed with an audience and goal in mind, can be used or consumed by people.

Teaching students how to produce information responsibly may better prepare them to become responsible information consumers.

Cybersafety

With the proliferation of instant messaging, cell phones, text messaging, and social networks, a rising concern of teachers, parents, and communities is the safety of our children as they travel the information superhighway. It is not a new concern. But as our children have rapidly outpaced many of their parents and teachers in the cultivation of their personal networks, we have become more fearful about the safety of our sons and daughters. On the other hand, it is crucial to note that while the popular media has recognized the issue as important, it has also staked a special claim on an issue that draws emotional attention, their bread and butter. By over emphasizing certain aspects and potentials of danger on the Internet, fear and even hysteria have resulted in an *ostrich in the sand* approach to net safety in many schools. It is an unfortunate and dangerous reaction. When we are prevented, by network filters and policies, from teaching our children how to play and work safely on the Internet, then children may not have the opportunity to learn about safe behaviors while online.

Recent studies have revealed that the Internet is far less dangerous than is popularly assumed. A 2007 study, sponsored by the National School Boards Association and conducted by Grunwall Associates indicates that:

> Students and parents report fewer recent or current problems, such as cyberstalking, cyberbullying, and unwelcome personal encounters, than school fears and policies seem to imply.

Inappropriate Exposure	Percent of Students	Percent of Parents
Children seeing inappropriate images online	20%	11%
Inappropriate language	18%	16%
Have been asked for personal identifying information	7%	6%
Experienced self-defined cyberbullying	7%	4%
Had conversations that made them uncomfortable	4%	3%
Unwelcome strangers have tried repeatedly to communicate	3%	3%
Had a stranger ask to meet them in person	2%	2%
Actually met someone in person without permission	0.08%	

Figure 5.4: NSBA Report

Figure 5.4 described some of the findings from the report's three surveys.

On the other hand, the NSBA study reports that 59 percent of online students say that they talk about education-related topics on their social networks, including college, college planning, learning outside of school, news, careers, politics, ideas, religion, morals, and schoolwork. Fifty percent say they talk specifically about school work.

In other words, students are much more likely to be discussing school work than engaged in personally dangerous behaviors when interacting in their social networks ("Creating & Connecting").

Neither this, nor the American Psychological Association's 2008 report, "Online 'Predators' and Their Victims: Myths, Realities and Implications for Prevention" should be cause to let our guards down completely. Inappropriate, unhealthy, and even dangerous content exists on the Internet. Cyberbullying is a common problem, and sexual predators do exist. However, as the APA report's press release states:

" ...students are much more likely to be discussing school work than engaged in personally dangerous behaviors.

> ...In spite of public concern, the authors found that adolescents' use of popular social networking sites such as MySpace and FaceBook do not appear to increase their risk of being victimized by online predators. Rather it is risky online interactions such as talking online about sex to unknown people that increases vulnerability, according to the researchers. (Mills)

The networks are not the risk. Risky behavior is the risk, and therefore it is imperative that cyber safety be a part of raising and educating our children, just like traffic safety.

Action Items

Directors of Technology

- Consider renaming your Acceptable Use Policy (AUP) to Ethics in Information Policy (EIP). Expand this document to include the ethical use of all information and information processing and delivery technologies.

- Consider establishing an EIP that is meaningful at an elementary school level, one for the middle school, and one for high schools. You might even consider a separate EIP for staff. Make them teachable documents, constructed so they can become a springboard for discussions about the ethical use of information.

- Work toward describing elements of the EIP as proactive ways of promoting meaningful use of technology, rather than exclusively in terms of limiting access. Think in terms of "Thou shall . . ." rather than "Thou shall not . . . ."

- Work with the central office supervisors of other content areas to integrate EIP practices into their curriculum work and professional development endeavors.

- Try to limit use of the term *technology* when discussing integration, staff development, and planning. Try to use the term *contemporary literacy* as much as possible, and utilize all opportunities to help people to understand a different vision or definition of what literacy is for our students.

- Establish staff development for teachers aimed at critical evaluation of Net-based and other information sources. Add online opportunities for the ongoing conversations about the appropriate use of digital networked content.

- Prepare a presentation about cybersafety, or hire a consultant to present on the subject to teachers, parents, and the community at any appropriate occasion. Make the presentation as proactive as possible. Avoid using scare tactics.

Principals and Head Teachers

- Make sure that the entire faculty understands the district's EIP or AUP and that all teachers are making their students clearly aware of their opportunities, responsibilities, and limitations.

- Make sure, during casual and formal evaluations, that all teachers are making use of a variety of information resources, and that they are encouraging students to question the ethical use of information sources that are available to them.

- Offer training to teachers and parents regarding cybersafety. Promote positive and productive uses of the Internet. Avoid stressing the fear factor. Work to make cybersafety an element of school culture.

Media Specialists

- Add a page to your media center Web site that points to Web tools designed to assist students (and teachers) in evaluating information resources and in crediting the owners/authors of the information.

- Provide casual professional development for teachers in evaluating and crediting information from the Internet and other resources.

- Work with students to make sure they understand how to evaluate and credit information resources.

- Provide materials and support related to cybersafety, and support it as an element of school culture.

School Tech Facilitators

- Assist the media specialist in establishing a Web page with links to Web tools designed to assist students (and teachers) in evaluating information resources and in crediting the owners/authors of the information.

- Provide other casual and formal professional development on evaluating and crediting information sources.

- Organize technology fairs for parents and community members, and use these opportunities to, among other things, help them understand the value of information is changing and, as a result, ethical issues need to be addressed.

- Work with the principal and media specialist to support cybersafety instruction in the classrooms and as an element of school culture.

Teachers

- Require that students cite all unoriginal information that is used in their information products.

- Require that students evaluate all unoriginal information that is used in their information products.

- Be willing to put students' selected information sources on trial, asking them to defend their usage of the information.

Students

- The information that you use to learn and to communicate is only as valuable as its truthfulness. Make sure it is truthful.

Parents

- Ask your children about information they find on the Internet or in magazines and reference books. Ask them why they think it is true and what the implications might be if it is not.

CHAPTER 6

Implementation

O ver recent months and years, there has been a dramatic increase in conversations about new skills in education circles. ISTE's recent NETS Refresh illustrates a shift from technology to information. The original NETS (National Education Technology Standards) emphasized:

- Basic Operations and Concepts
- Social, Ethical, and Human Issues
- Technology Productivity Tools
- Technology Communications Tools
- Technology Research Tools
- Technology Problem-solving and Decision-making Tools

The new NETS ask for curriculum that teaches:

- Creativity and Innovation
- Communication and Collaboration
- Research and Information Fluency
- Critical Thinking, Problem Solving, and Decision Making

> **''** ...that we start to explicitly talk about literacy as learning literacies – the basic skills involved in helping yourself learn what you need to know to do what you need to do. **''**

- Digital Citizenship
- Technology Operations and Concepts

The relative omission of technology and tools in the new version of technology skills is conspicuous, and calls for a shift from technology fluency as the goal to information fluency. We are realizing that teaching technology today would make as much sense as teaching pencil was in the 1950s and '60s. The shifts in our information landscape have impacted on society and caused us to rethink what and how we teach, not advances in technology.

Figure 6.1 in simple terms, a rethinking of literacy.

Traditional Literacy Goals		Contemporary Literacy Goals
Literacy	→	Learning Literacy
Literacy Skills	→	Literacy Habits
Lifelong Learning	→	Learning Lifestyle

Figure 6.1: Shifts

There is a popular projection that is touted at education technology conferences—that today's students will hold, on the average, 10.2 jobs from ages 18 to 38. It is one of those "Aha!" statements that, when truly considered and researched, has less impact when we learn that almost half of those jobs happen between the ages of 18 and 22 (U.S. Bureau of Labor Statistics). We all held numerous summer and pocket change jobs in high school and college.

Yet we see evidence of changing work environments and geographic shifts of entire industries all around us. There were 16 textile mills that employed thousands of the inhabitants of my home town. They are all gone today. And as most of our jobs depend on working information, and the information and communication technologies continue to advance, there is little doubt that continual learning has become, and will remain to be, a major part of prospering in the coming decades.

If we accept that learning is a predominant part of today and tomorrow's work and lifestyle, then perhaps we should rethink literacy and start to explicitly talk about literacy for learning, or *learning literacy*. If learning becomes the clear aim of literacy, and not focused so exclusively on literacy skills to be taught and checked off, then *literacy habits*,

practiced every day in every lesson, will become the outcome of our classroom experiences, and we and our students will come to embrace a *learning lifestyle*.

There are three basic ways that we can help children develop learning literacy habits for a learning lifestyle:

1. Learning in the New Information Landscape

There continues to be a sense that the jury is still out regarding one to one (1:1) learning—each student having ubiquitous access to a computer and the Internet. Articles such as the May 4, 2007, *New York Times* story "Seeing No Progress, Some Schools Drop Laptops," give naysayers excuses to impede progress.

> The students at Liverpool High have used their school-issued laptops to exchange answers on tests, download pornography and hack into local businesses. When the school tightened its network security, a 10th grader not only found a way around it but also posted step-by-step instructions on the Web for others to follow (which they did). (Hu)

This and similar articles tell us that technology alone is not an answer. In fact, I often urge audiences that they should "Stop integrating technology!" We have to think differently about teaching and learning, not simply use new tools. But these technologies, computers, software, and the Internet, are the pencil and paper of our time.

If we are going to prepare our children to responsibly prosper in today's information environment, then we need to teach them from today's information environment. It means that they learn from information that is networked, digital, and overwhelming, that we alter pedagogies for information-abundant learning environments, and that learners and teachers have convenient access to information at all times.

Perhaps because of the growing conversations about 21st century skills, the number of students who are entering their classrooms with laptops under their arms is growing. According to the 2006 American Digital Schools report, only 4 percent of U.S. school districts had started 1:1 implementations in 2003. In 2006, it increased to 24 percent of districts reporting to be "in the process of transitioning to 1:1."

More schools are equipping their classrooms with permanently mounted digital projectors and interactive white boards. This is sparked, in no small part, by enormous investments by the United Kingdom for interactive white boards, classroom projectors, and a new requirement that all classrooms implement virtual learning environments.

British readers of this book will caution us that they still have many challenges to overcome. But a growing realization that students need to learn from today's information landscape was illustrated magnificently when attendees at the annual NAACE conference in Torquay, England, were addressed by Jim Knight, the nation's Minister of State for Schools, from SecondLife, a Multi User Virtual Environment (M.U.V.E.). (See Figure 6.2: Speech from Second Life)

Figure 6.2: Speech from Second Life

Alan Kay is attributed to defining technology as "anything that was invented after you were born." For our children, it is their pencil and paper, and learning without computers and the Internet is as relevant as my learning with clay tablets.

2. Learning within New Conversations

Simply adding information technologies to the classroom is not nearly enough to accomplish a retooling for contemporary literacy. The most important instruction will happen not as fingers touch the machine, but as spoken words

Web Resources

SecondLife – http://secondlife.com/

are exchanged. Some teachers continue to resist Wikipedia as a source for information. Its value is in the conversations that it inspires.

"What do you learn about this topic from the Wikipedia?"
"How do you know it is true?"

Traditionally, we were taught to assume the authority of the information that we encountered in school. We were taught to use textbooks and the reference books to seek the answers to questions, sources that we could rely on, and this was not the wrong approach in an information-scarce learning environment.

However, today, we should stop teaching students to assume authority, and, instead, teach them to prove the authority. If a teacher stands in front of his class and says, "The world is like this." Then that teacher is still teaching students to assume authority. If the teacher stands in front of the class and says, "According to this source, which is reliable for these reasons, the world is like this." Then that teacher is teaching that part of what they are learning is the evidence that what they are learning is true. This is contemporary literacy, and teachers should talk about contemporary literacy with every lesson.

Proving authority would also be part of each student's responsibility. They should be accustomed to having their teachers point to their writing or their presentations and asking, "How do you know that is true?" If they cannot satisfactorily answer that question, then they lose points, even if the information is true.

Of course, this challenge could as easily be turned around. Students should be able to interrupt their teachers, during their lecture, and ask, "But Mrs. Hobgood, how do you know that is true?" and Mrs. Hobgood needs to be able to convincingly answer that question.

There are many more examples, but it is urgent that teachers bring as much networked digital content into the classroom, so they have the opportunity to say, "I found this information in this way, asked myself these questions in determining its appropriateness, and altered it in these ways to add value."

We cannot simply teach literacy. We have to talk about exposing what is true, employing information, expressing ideas compellingly, and using information ethically. It must be part of our conversations.

3. Modeling the Learning Lifestyle

If we accept that developing lifelong learning skills should be part of our students' classroom experiences, then the most effective way that we can promote this as habit is to model a learning lifestyle. This means that when asked a question by a student, teachers and librarians should be willing and even eager to say, "I do not know the answer to that question. How do you think we might go about finding the answer?" Today, this is an appropriate answer, even if the answer is known.

This practice exemplifies a saying attributed to social writer Eric Hoffer.

> In times of change learners inherit the earth, while the learned find themselves beautifully equipped to work in a world that no longer exists.

Teachers and librarians should talk with their students about what they are learning. We should bring something new into every class, something that we have just learned. We should talk about how we are learning and why we continue to learn.

Modeling ourselves as master learners also gives us permission to ask our students, "How did you get your Web page to do that?"

One often stated (and unstated) reason why some teachers are reluctant to use information and communication technologies in front of their students is the fear of appearing to be less knowledgeable about something than their students. Instead of avoiding using something we are not comfortable with, we should demonstrate our willingness to learn, and openly respect our students' knowledge and skills.

A growing community of educators is practicing and celebrating their own learning as part of being educators.

Personal Learning Networks

The Internet started as an almost exclusively collaborative environment. E-mail and mailing lists were used for communication long before the advent of the World Wide Web. E-mail enabled personal communication, but mailing lists facilitated the formation of communities around professional and personal interests. These communities of interest usually required a central figure with the technical skills to install and configure the mailing list software, or access to the required expertise. Because of the technical attention required for the formation and maintenance of these communities, they remained fairly focused on a particular area of interest. They became, in a sense, a room for conversation, a container.

Many years later—and several years ago—we were building portals, Web sites that were larger structures with lots of rooms for conversation. A school district might establish a portal with rooms for librarians, rooms for elementary school teachers, principals, social studies teachers, and various other working committees. There was a common place where members could login, and their usernames would give them access to the specific rooms of conversation and resources appropriate for the user.

During recent years, three conditions have risen that are changing online communities.

First of all, the Internet has become, once again, a highly collaborative environment. Blogging has given voice to individuals, regardless of technical expertise and expense. Out of this spirit of information democracy has risen a sense that the Internet should be a place to not merely consume content, but to share and grow knowledge.

The second condition comes from the growth of open source applications and platforms. Because of the freedom to alter and adapt socially supported applications, and free and evolving platforms like the Apache Web server, PHP programming language, and MYSQL database software, a growing community of developers has created and launched a bewildering array of inventive collaborative Internet applications.

Finally, an underlying foundation of new connectivity, RSS, has enabled us to combine many of these new applications and the content that flows through and out of them. We find ourselves almost spontaneously forming networks that connect us to people and resources that help us do our jobs. The descriptive term that has risen out of conversations about these new connections and the communities they enable us to cultivate is *Personal Learning Networks*.

There is certainly nothing new about personal learning networks. We have always surrounded ourselves with people we can converse with, libraries for research, and personal books for quick reference. We've subscribed to magazines, journals, and newspapers and kept PBS and The Learning Network among our favorite TV channels. However, in a time of rapid change, we need our networks to extend beyond our geographic locations and pre-programmed broadcasting.

At the time of this writing, I am sitting at a local Starbucks coffee shop (walkable from my house), connected to the Internet through a mobile broadband card. While describing personal learning networks in this article, I received a community Twitter message from Steve Dembo, who was getting ready to start a presentation for educators in Buck County, Pennsylvania. Mr. Dembo announced that he would be broadcasting the presentation through USTREAM, a Web-based personal broadcasting tool. So, with ear buds applied, I watched and listened to the presentation about digital natives and digital immigrants as I continued to write this chapter on personal learning through networks.

USTREAM features a chat screen, where the 39 other educators who were watching from a distance (including virtual attendees from Perth, Australia and another from Shanghai, China) could discuss what Steve is saying. Through the chat, we talked about how time zones have become the important boundary of our time, in many ways more significant than national boundaries and even language and culture.

This book will likely take months to publish after the final draft is submitted. The author's blog is published immediately. In a time of rapid change, as books remain an essential route for learning, immediate and distant communications are increasingly a critical means for us to learn, adapt, and prosper. Figure 6.3 is a rough diagram of my personal learning network.

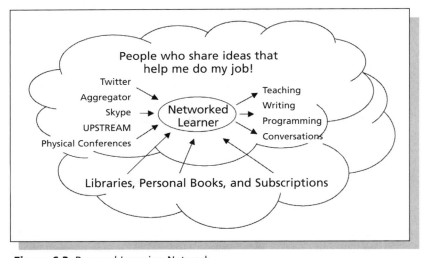

Figure 6.3: Personal Learning Network

The cloud represents a universe of information that comes from formally published content and more casual conversations among people who are teachers, learners, credentialed experts, passionate hobbyists, consultants, business people, scientists, librarians, philosophers, and more. They contribute to learning from all over North America to Lima, Bogotá, London, Edinburgh, Barcelona, Dubai, Hong Kong, Shanghai, Perth, Sidney, and Christchurch, to mention only a few of the known connections. We are facing many of the same challenges from different perspectives, and through conversations and by cultivating our personal learning networks, we are crossing many barriers to accomplishing progressive and productive education.

Tips for Cultivating Your Personal Learning Network

Finding contributors to your personal learning network is fairly easy. Once started, it is more difficult to prune. Starting with a limited number of bloggers who are saying things that help you do your job is prudent. There are two good Web pages to visit to find those first few (or many) edubloggers to start with.

Bloggers to Learn From—This is a Wiki page where a community of educators has collaborated to compile a categorized list of favorite edubloggers.

Education Blogger List—This is a list compiled by LiveMocha blogger Aseem Badshah. It is an ordered list based on each blogger's **Technorati's Authority Index**, a value calculated from the number of other bloggers who link to the listed blog. Will Richardson's Weblogg-ed is at the top of the list with an index of 925. Stephen's Web from Stephen Downes ranks number two (index of 792), because slightly fewer bloggers link to his publication.

When you have subscribed to your starting bloggers (with your aggregator) and begun to read their articles, you will likely notice that they often write about other bloggers. You will learn about other practitioners who are reflecting on their experience, and you will begin to pay attention to some of them as well, as you continue to grow your network.

Many bloggers include in the sidebar of their blog page a section called the blogroll. This is a list of the bloggers they read regularly. If you find a particular writer who is contributing to your learning, then the people they pay attention to may also be worthy of your reading.

Twitter is another potent avenue for personal learning. Many edubloggers include on their blog pages a link to their Twitter page. As you visit their Twitter page, you will see the latest Tweets they have published, short statements that cannot exceed 140 characters—microblogs, if you will. If you see value in what they are writing, then you can set up your own Twitter account, and then click **Follow** on their twitter page so that every time they Tweet, the message comes to you.

Web Resources

Bloggers to Learn From – http://snurl.com/23szh
Education Blogger List – http://snurl.com/23t00
Weblogg-ed – http://weblogg-ed.com/
Stephen's Web – http://downes.ca/

Twitter deserves special consideration, because it is a difficult concept to explain. Often, when it is described well, the immediate response is, "Why would I ever want to do that?" However, when experienced, Twitter's value becomes apparent as you find yourself forming a community of learning. It works like this.

1. You set up an account.

2. Then you find someone to start following. You are welcome to start with me (http://twitter.com/dwarlick/). Go to my page and click **Follow**.

3. When I post a Twitter message, it comes to your Twitter page and the pages of others who follow me. As you post a Twitter message, it goes to all of the people who have selected to follow you. In a very real way, this is like micro-blogging.

In the sidebar of my Twitter page, you will see a grid of icons for the Twitter users I am paying attention to (34 at the moment). Click them to see what they are saying and whom they are following. If you like what you read, then click to Follow them.

Most Twits (Common term for Twitter users) use an application to monitor their Twitter network, rather than having their Twitter Web page opened. There are numerous Firefox extensions, but many people use applications, such as Twitterific and Twirl. They run in the background and notify you when a message comes in.

Often, Twitter messages come from a conference presenter, announcing that she is preparing to deliver a presentation, and that it will be USTREAM'ed. Several weeks ago, I was delivering an address at the Houston Chapter of the American Leadership Forum to an audience of educators, education leaders, school board members, and representatives from the local business community. Texas educator Stephanie Sandifer brought two video cameras and used her computer to broadcast the presentation through USTREAM. She announced the broadcast through Twitter and ended with 58 observers from around the globe. Virtual attendees even contributed to the Q&A after the address, a melding of the physical and virtual learning experience.

Tips for Pruning Your Personal Learning Network

If you establish a personal learning network, find value in it, and grow your network, you will eventually feel like you are inside the NASA Control Space Center, coordinating the landing of 12 space shuttles all by yourself. You can find yourself in the middle of an avalanche of information and wonder how you ever got there. In truth, we are attempting to land our students on the moon. But it doesn't have to feel that way, if we can control our learning networks.

Web Resourcess

Twitter – http://twitter.com/

- Controlling our PLNs is not something that any of us are really good at yet, but there are ways that we might work toward a more manageable flow of information.

- Try to hold yourself to a limit of bloggers you are subscribing to. It may be 10, 20, or 30—whatever feels comfortable. But do not make it an uncrossable line. You may discover, with experience, that you can follow more than 10 bloggers.

- Set up folders in your aggregator based on frequency of reading. Call one folder "Everyday," and in it, place blogs and news sources that you need to follow every day. Call another one "Once a Week," and load it with less critical postings.

- It's okay to switch Twitter off every once in a while. We're actually pretty smart as individuals, and sometimes we just have to sift through what we've learned and what we believe and make that work for us—just do it ourselves. While Twitter is still off, take a break, go for a walk, or a bicycle ride. Go visit a neighbor or just walk around in your garden for a few minutes.

- It is okay to ignore other parts of your PLN when you need to. Your aggregator will wait for you. It may start to burst at the seams, but it won't explode (at least no one's ever been physically injured).

- Scan! It is possible that you may only actually read one in 10 of the blogs that come through, depending on who you are aggregating.

- Your aggregator can grow temporary limbs. If you are teaching a brand new unit, or have been asked to deliver a presentation you have not done before, find people whose writings will help you prepare and subscribe to them. When you've learned what you need, then sever the lines.

- Realize that your network is much larger than it seems, much larger than the ones you've directly connected to, because you are not just reading single bloggers, but all of the bloggers that he or she is reading. We are like a giant sieve, each of us sifting through information and ideas, adding to them, reshaping them, and each of us judging their relevance and usefulness. It's bigger than you think. It's more valuable than you think. It is more treacherous than you think. Limit your network with this in mind!

- Another way to gauge the practicality of your PLN is to set for yourself the amount of time you can give up to scanning your aggregator. David Jakes said, during a virtual presentation the other day, "Are you willing to spend 15 minutes a day learning?" If you find that after 15 minutes you are still not getting to all of the connections you need, then you can consider a different strategy.

- You do not need to subscribe to dozens of educators to learn how they are using VoiceThread. Instead, conduct a Google Blog Search for voicethread, and then subscribe to the search RSS feed. If anyone blogs about VoiceThread, their blog comes to your aggregator. Another search tool you might use in the same way is Technorati.

- Some bloggers are very good connectors and filters. They read lots of information, and then blog the gems. An excellent example is OLDaily, by Stephen Downes (D. Warlick).

This type of hyper-connectivity between educators and their world is important today. Connecting beyond the walls of our libraries and classrooms is critical, as we work to provide education for today's children and their future. These networks are potent for three important reasons.

1. They geographically extend our network of information access and knowledge.

2. They allow people to connect to each other, not simply because they are physically close to each other geographically or culturally, but they connect through their ideas.

3. These networks are personal. We craft and cultivate them for ourselves, to help us do our jobs and accomplish our goals.

Action Items

Directors of Technology

- Think of and talk about your Acceptable Use Policy (AUP) as if it were called your Ethics in Information Policy (EIP). Expand your AUP to include the ethical use of all information, and information processing and delivery technologies.

- Consider establishing AUPs that are meaningful for elementary school students, middle school students, and one for high schools. You might even consider a separate AUP for staff.

- Work toward describing elements of the AUP as proactive ways of promoting meaningful use of technology, rather than exclusively in terms of limiting access. Think in terms of "Thou shall . . ." rather than "Thou shall not . . . ."

- Work with the central office supervisors of other content areas to integrate AUP practices and guidelines into their curriculum work and professional development endeavors.

Web Resources

Voicethread – http://voicethread.com
Technorati – http://technorati.com/
OLDaily – http://downes.ca/news/OLDaily.htm

- Try to limit your use of the term technology when discussing integration, staff development, and planning. Try to use the term contemporary literacy as much as possible and utilize all opportunities to help people understand a different vision or definition of what literacy is for our students.

- Establish staff development for teachers aimed at responsible use of intellectual property, critical evaluation of content, and proactive protection of the district's information infrastructure.

Principals

- Make sure the entire faculty understands the district's AUP and that all teachers are making their students clearly aware of their opportunities, responsibilities, and limitations.

- Make sure, during casual and formal evaluations, that all teachers are making use of a variety of information resources, and they are encouraging students through instruction and example to make ethical use of information, both digital and print.

Media Specialists

- Add a page to your media center Web site that points to Web tools designed to assist students (and teachers) in making appropriate use of intellectual property, critically evaluating information resources, and protecting the school and district's information infrastructure.

- Establish a Web page that helps students and families practice safe and productive use of computers and the Internet.

- Provide casual professional development for teachers in evaluating and crediting information from the Internet and other resources.

- Work with students to make sure they understand how to evaluate and credit information resources.

School Tech Facilitators

- Assist the media specialist in establishing a Web page with links to Web tools designed to assist students (and teachers) in evaluating information resources and in crediting the owners/authors of the information.

- Assist the school media specialist in establishing a Web page that helps students and families practice safe and productive use of computers and the Internet.

- Provide other casual and formal professional development on evaluating and crediting information sources.

- Organize technology fairs for parents and community members, and use these opportunities to, among other things, help them understand that the value of information is changing, and, as a result, ethical issues need to be addressed.

Teachers

- Require that students cite all unoriginal information that is used in their information products.

- Require that students evaluate all unoriginal information that is used in their information products.

- Be willing to put students' selected information sources on trial, asking them to defend their usage of the information.

Students

- The information you use to learn and to communicate is only as valuable as its truthfulness. Make sure it is truthful.

Parents

- Ask your children about information they find on the Internet or in magazines and reference books. Ask them why they think it is true and what the implications might be if it is not.

CHAPTER 7

Conclusion

Becoming Resourceful Learners

Several years ago I worked as a consultant for ThinkQuest, an educational project created by Advanced Network and Services. Al Weis, the organization's president, wanted to create an opportunity for students to learn not only technical skills associated with the growing Internet, but also to learn other disciplines within an increasingly digital and connected world.

ThinkQuest was a revolutionary project, because in 1995 most teachers had never seen the World Wide Web. This contest had teams of students collaborating to create Web sites, and they were competing for scholarships and fame. However, at a deeper and more relevant level, ThinkQuest was an experience within which students explored and mastered contemporary literacy skills. They learned to expose the value within their information experience: finding relevant information, decoding and evaluating it, and organizing the information into valuable libraries of useful content. They learned to employ their information: analyzing, processing, manipulating, and adding value to the knowledge they gained. And finally, these teams of students learned to express their ideas compellingly through text, images, animation, sound, video, and virtual environments.

Each year, Advanced Network & Services, the originators of ThinkQuest, hold a ThinkQuest weekend where a final level of judging takes place and the final awards are presented, more than a million dollars in scholarships. In my association with ThinkQuest, I was able to attend a number of these events, each in a major city.

At the end of the second year, this culminating event was held in Washington, D.C. at a swanky hotel off of the capital mall. On the second afternoon, each team was provided a state-of-the-art computer, high-speed connection to the Internet, and asked to demonstrate and discuss their Web sites with visitors from across the city. It was highly illuminating to see what these high school students had accomplished and learned in the process. Everyone was appropriately impressed.

By the end of the afternoon, I had visited and spoken with most of the teams, but just before leaving, I noticed a computer in the corner with a poster above it that displayed in gothic script *The Middle Ages*. There was only one youngster at the computer. His partners had obviously left since it was the end of the session. I walked over to the station ready to talk some history. After all, I had taught history for nearly 10 years, and I thought I would educate him a bit. As it turned out, he educated me, a humbling experience. What amazed me about this young man's knowledge was not his command of the major events and trends of those centuries, but what he had learned about the nuances of the lives of the people who lived there: how they had fun, the work they did, their festivals, how the casts interacted with each other, and more.

I finally asked the youngster how old he was, and he responded, "15."

Then I asked where he had learned about the Middle Ages, to which he responded, "from college professors."

I asked again how old he was, just in case I had misunderstood. Having not misheard his answer, I asked how he had arranged to learn about the Middle Ages from college professors. He explained how, when he had identified something that he needed to learn, he would visit university Web sites, looking for courses that probably taught it. Then he would send an e-mail message to the professor of the course asking questions that would evoke the answers he needed. Brilliant! Then the boy explained that he never told the professors he was only 15. He told them he was a graduate assistant doing research. He got his answers.

As I finally walked away, his teacher caught up with me, tapped me on the shoulder, and explained that the young man I had been talking to was not a successful student, that he had been at risk of failing core subjects, and had a generally poor attitude about school. She explained that he had blossomed as a result of this project and had exhibited not only an eagerness to learn, but also leadership skills that had never been apparent before.

It is my opinion that what this young man learned as a result of his participation in ThinkQuest was as important, if not more so, than what his classmates were learning who were making good grades. He had learned to make himself an expert, and he and his classmates will be doing this for the rest of their lives. If our children are ready for their future, it will be because they know how to teach themselves. It will be because they have learned to resourcefully use their information environment, to help themselves learn what they need to know, to do what they need to do, when they need to do it.

At the heart of being a lifelong self-educating person is a literacy that is relevant to our time and the information that surrounds us. It means that we cannot only read the information that someone hands to us, but that we can investigate and expose what is true and valuable about the information. It means that we can add, subtract, count, measure, and calculate numbers. But it also means that we can employ the information that we have found to answer questions, solve problems, and accomplish goals, adding to our personal and community experiences. Not only can we write, but we also can use images, sound, video, animation, and text to express our ideas in ways that affect other people—that help them help us accomplish our goals.

> " If our children are ready for their future, it will be because they have learned to resourcefully use their information environment, to help themselves learn what they need to know, to do what they need to do, when they need to do it. "

Finally, lifelong learners must know how to use information responsibly and within a context that is shared by other people. In a world that is increasingly driven by information, its ethical use is critical to helping our friends, communities, and world improve its condition.

Now it is your turn. I have given you a variety of suggestions, or action items to consider in your own working environment. These are not intended to be a firm guideline, but suggestions for ways that various stakeholders might further the modernization of schools and classrooms. Consider them and use those that fit well with your circumstances.

I also want to urge you to talk back to me and other readers of this book. Go to the Web site at:

http://davidwarlick.com/redefining_literacy/

Here you will be able to comment on aspects of this book that impress you in some way and discuss with others and myself where we might go to further promote a new literacy for the 21st century.

Thank you!

Appendix A: Other Suggested Works—Books

Digital Literacy, by Paul Gilster. John Wiley & Sons. 1997. ISBN 0471165204

Literacy in a Digital World: Teaching and Learning in the Age of Information, by Kathleen Tyner. Lawrence Erlbaum Assoc. 1998. ISBN 0805822267

Learning Right from Wrong in the Digital Age: An Ethics Guide for Parents, Teachers, Librarians, and Others Who Care about Computer-Using Young People, by Doug Johnson. Linworth Publishing Company. 2003. ISBN 1586831313

Growing Up Digital, by Don Tapscot. McGraw-Hill Trade. 1999. ISBN 0071347984

Being Digital, by Nicolas Negroponte. Alfred A. Knopf. 1995. ISBN 0679762906

Adolescents and Literacies in a Digital World (New Literacies and Digital Epistemologies, Vol. 7), Edited by Donna E. Alvermann. Peter Lang Publishing. 2002. ISBN 0820455733

Teaching TV Production in a Digital World: Integrating Media Literacy, by Robert Kenny. Libraries Unlimited. 2001. ISBN 156308726X

The Director in the Classroom, by Nikos Theodosakis. Tech4Learning, Inc. 2001. ISBN 1930870116

Beyond Technology: Questioning, Research and the Information Literate School, by Jamie McKenzie. FNO Press. 2000. ISBN 0967407826

Empowering Students with Technology, by Alan November. Corwin Press. 2001. ISBN 1575173727

Ethics in School Librarianship: A Reader, by Carol Simpson. Linworth Publishing, Inc. 2003. ISBN 1586830848

Learning Right from Wrong in the Digital Age, by Doug Johnson. Linworth Publishing, Inc. 2003. ISBN 1586831313

Thinking in the Future Tense, by Jennifer James. Free Press. 1997. ISBN 0684832690

The Next Fifty Years: Science in the First Half of the Twenty-First Century, Edited by John Brockman. Vintage Books. 2002. ISBN 0375713425

Millennials Rising, by Neil Howe & William Strauss. Vintage Books. 2000. ISBN 0375707190

Catalog of Tomorrow: Trends Shaping your Future, Edited by Andrew Zolli. TechTV. 2002. ISBN 0789728109

Appendix B: Other Suggested Works—Web Documents

Report: Digital literacy is essential for students
<http://eschoolnews.com/news/showStory.cfm?ArticleID=3592>
Digital Literacy: Re-Thinking Education and Training in a Digital World
<http://digitalliteracy.mwg.org/>
A Primer on Digital Literacy
<http://horizon.unc.edu/projects/resources/digital_literacy.asp>
A New Digital Literacy: A Conversation with Paul Gilster <http://ascd.org/readin-groom/edlead/9711/pool.html>
More than Access <http://educause.edu/pub/er/erm00/articles006/erm0063.pdf>
The Literacy Web (at the University of Connecticut) <http://literacy.uconn.edu/>
Digital Transformation: A Framework for ICT Literacy
<http://ets.org/search97cgi/s97_cgi>
The Importance of Contemporary Literacy in the Digital Age: A Response to Digital
Transformation: A Framework for ICT Literacy
<http://cosn.org/resources/051402.htm>

Appendix C : Where to Find the Future

The Media Lab—http://media.mit.edu/
Xerox PARC—http://parc.xerox.com/
Institute of NanoTechnology—http://nano.org.uk/
IBM Research—http://researchweb.watson.ibm.com/
Technology Review—http://technologyreview.com/
SlashDot: News for Nerds—http://slashdot.org/
TechDirt—http://techdirt.com
SciTech—http://scitech.com
IT Conversations Podcasts—http://itc.conversationsnetwork.org/
Pop Tech—http://poptech.com/
TED—http://ted.com/

Appendix D : Creative Commons Designations

Attribution. You let others copy, distribute, display, and perform your copyrighted work—and derivative works based upon it—but only if they give credit the way you request.

Noncommercial. You let others copy, distribute, display, and perform your work—and derivative works based upon it—but for noncommercial purposes only.

No Derivative Works. You let others copy, distribute, display, and perform only verbatim copies of your work, not derivative works based upon it.

Share Alike. You allow others to distribute derivative works only under a license identical to the license that governs your work ("About: License Your Work").

Works Cited

"About." *Creative Commons*. 24 Mar. 2008. 26 Mar. 2008
   <http://creativecommons.org/about/>.

"About: License Your Work." *Creative Commons*. 2008. 2 Jan. 2008 <http://creativecommons.org/about/license/>.

"About Us." *TeacherTube*. TeacherTube LLC. 2008. 18 Jan. 2008 <http://teachertube.com/about.php>.

"America's Digital Schools 2006: A Five-Year Forecast." *America's Digital Schools 2007*. 2006. The Greaves Group. 1 Apr. 2008
   <http://ads2006.net/ads2006/pdf/ADS2006KF.pdf>.

"Are They Really Ready to Work?" *Partnership for 21st Century Skills*. 2006. The Conference Board, Partnership for 21st Century Skills, Corporate Voices for Working Families, and Society for Human Resource Management. 12 Aug. 2008
   <http://21stcenturyskills.org/documents/FINAL_REPORT_PDF09-29-06.pdf>.

Bauder, David. "Decline in TV Viewership Has the Networks Worried." *Deseret News* [Salt Lake City] 9 May 2007: A02.

"Broadband Meets Broadcast." *informitv News*. 4 Feb. 2007. informitv. 16 Jan. 2008
   <http://informitv.com/articles/2007/02/04/youtubeviewerswatch/>.

Burns, Enid. "Top 10 Search Providers, July 2007." *Search Engine Watch*. 30 Aug. 2007. Incisive Interactive Marketing LLC. 8 Sept. 2007
   <http://searchenginewatch.com/showPage.html?page=3626903>.

"Cell Phone Boom in Rural Africa." *World News/Africa*. 4 Oct. 2006. MSNBC. 9 Apr. 2008 <http://msnbc.msn.com/id/15129709/>.

Claburn, Thomas. "Viruses, Spyware, Phishing Cost U.S. Consumers $7 Billion Over Two Years." *InformationWeek*. 6 Aug. 2007. United Business Media LLC. 29 Mar. 2008
   <http://informationweek.com/story/showArticle.jhtml?articleID=201203030>.

"Community Connections." *Moyers on America*. 2006. PBS. 18 Jan. 2008
   <http://pbs.org/moyers/moyersonamerica/net/community.html>.

"Creating & Connecting/Research and Guidelines on Online Social—and Educational—Networking." *NSBA*. July 2007. National School Boards Association. 30 Mar. 2008
   <http://nsba.org/SecondaryMenu/TLN/CreatingandConnecting.aspx>.

Dembo, Steve. iChat interview. 11 Sept. 2007.

"Executive Summary." *How Much Information?* 2003. 27 Oct. 2003. Regents of the University of California. 11 Apr. 2008
   <www2.sims.berkeley.edu/research/projects/how-much-info-2003/ execsum.htm/>.

"Framework for 21st Century Learning." *The Partnership for 21st Century Skills*. 30 July 2007. 5 Sept. 2007
   <http://21stcenturyskills.org/index.php?option=com_content&task=view&id=254&Itemid=120>.

Friensen, Janice. "Giving Students 21st Century Skills: A Practical Guide to Contemporary Literacy." *MultiMedia Schools* 10 (2003): 22-31.

Geiger, Keith "Christa's legacy lives on." *NEA Today*. Feb. 1996. FindArticles.com. 12 Aug. 2008.
    <http://findarticles.com/p/articles/mi_qa3617/is_199602/ai_n8753649>.

Geoff, Duncan. "Get Around in Flickr Places." *Digital Trends*. 19 Nov. 2007. 18 Dec. 2007
    <http://news.digitaltrends.com/news/story/14864/get_around_in_flickr_places>.

Gilster, Paul. "A Look at What's Next." *The News & Observer*. 8 Jan. 2003. The McClatchy Company. 26 July 2008 <http://newsobserver.com/business/technology/gilster/2003/story/244024.html>.

Gomes, Lee. "Will All of Us Get Our 15 Minutes on a YouTube Video?" *The Wall Street Journal*. 30 Aug. 2006. 6 Jan. 2007 <http://online.wsj.com/public/article/SB115689298168048904-
    5wWyrSwyn6RfVfz9NwLk774VUWc_20070829.html?mod=rss_free>.

Gunn, Moira. "John Beck: When Gamers Enter the Workforce." [Podcast Tech Nation] 15 Mar. 2005. ITConversations. 9 Apr. 2008 <http://itc.conversationsnetwork.org/shows/detail436.html>.

Hammersley, Ben. "Audible Revolution." *The Guardian*. 2 Feb. 2004. Guardian News and Media Limited. 3 Jan. 2007
    <http://arts.guardian.co.uk/features/story/0,,1145758,00.html>.

Hancock, Hugh, and Johnnie Ingram. *Machinima for Dummies*. Indianapolis, IN: Wiley Publishing, Inc., 2007.

"Highest Degree Earned, Years of Full-Time Teaching Experience, and Average Class Size for Teachers in Public Elementary and Secondary Schools, by State: 2003-2004." *National Center for Education Statistics*. July 2006. U.S. Department of Education. 9 Sept. 2007
    <http://nces.ed.gov/programs/digest/d06/tables/dt06_064.asp>.

Hu, Winnie. "Seeing No Progress, Some Schools Drop Laptops." *The New York Times*. 4 May 2007. 5 May 2007 <http://nytimes.com/2007/05/04/education/04laptop.html>.

"ISTE NETS Refresh Project." *ISTE*. International Society for Technology Education. 5 Sept. 2007
    <http://iste.org/Content/NavigationMenu/NETS/NETS_Refresh_Forum/
    NETS_Refresh_.htm>.

Jakes, David. "Making a Case for Digital Storytelling." *TechLearning*. 1 Dec. 2005. Technology & Learning Magazine. 21 Dec. 2007
    <http://techlearning.com/story/showArticle.php?articleID=174401140>.

Jakes, David. "Rethinking Schools: Questions to Ask." *21st Century Connections*. 11 Mar. 2008. Technology & Learning. 21 June 2008
    <21centuryconnections.com/node/456>.

James, Jennifer. "Thinking in the Future Tense: Leadership for a New Age." 2002 Technology Leadership Academy. Pennsylvania Department of Education. The Penn Stater Conference Center Hotel, Pennsylvania. 9 July 2002.

Jennings, Richi. "Spam and Other Email Threats: Market and Technology Update." *Ferris Research*. 8 June 2007. 9 June 2007 <http://ferris.com/?p=315435>.

Johnson, Doug. *Learning Right from Wrong in the Digital Age*. Worthington, OH: Linworth Publishing, Inc., 2003.

Jones, Pamela. "Creative Commons License Upheld by Dutch Court." [Weblog Groklaw] 16 Mar. 2006. 29 Mar. 2008 <http://groklaw.net/article.php?story=20060316052623594>.

Kerr, Roger. "Hard-Headed Spending Decisions Not Cold-Hearted." *BusinessROUNDTABLE*. 2 July 2004. New Zealand Business Roundtable. 9 June 2007 <http://nzbr.org.nz/documents/articles/articles-2004/040702Copenhagen.htm>.

Kim, Ryan. "More Americans Go for Cell Phones, Drop Landlines." *San Francisco Chronicle*. 15 May 2007 A1. 23 July 2008 <http://sfgate.com/cgi-bin/artcle. cgi?f=/c/a/2007/05/15/MNGMOPR2HE1.DTL>.

Lauer, Tim. "Scuttle: Open Source Social Bookmarking Tool." [Weblog Education/Technology] 24 Jan. 2006. Lewis Elementary School. 12 Sept. 2007 <http://timlauer.org/2006/01/24/scuttle-open-source-social-bookmarking-tool/>.

Lenhart, Amanda, Mary Madden, Alexandra Rankin Macgill, and Aaron Smith. "Teens and Social Media." *PEW Internet & American Life Project*. 19 Dec. 2007. Pew Charitable Trusts. 20 Dec. 2007 <http://pewinternet.org/PPF/r/230/report_display.asp>.

"March 2008 Web Server Survey." *NetCraft*. 26 Mar. 2008. NetCraft LTD. 12 Apr. 2008 <http://news.netcraft.com/archives/2008/03/26/march_2008_web_server_survey.html>.

Markoff, John. "American Assistance for Cambodia." *Sweatshops and Butterflies: Cultural Ecology on the Edge*. 7 Aug. 2000. AAfC. 9 Apr. 2008 <http://camnet.com.kh/cambodiaschools/press_clippin.htm>.

Maxim, Kelly. "Camera Phones to De-Throne the Digital Camera?" *The Register*. 14 Feb. 2007. 20 Dec. 2007 <http://theregister.co.uk/2007/02/14/camera_phones_ascendant/>.

McCarthy, Wil. "Ultimate Alchemy." *WIRED Magazine*. 10 Sept. 2001. 11 Apr. 2008 <http://wired.com/wired/archive/9.10/atoms_pr.html>.

Mills, Kim. "'Internet Predator' Stereotypes Debunked in New Study." *APA Online*. 18 Feb. 2008. American Psychological Association. 21 Feb. 2008 <http://apa.org/releases/sexoffender0208.html>.

Mokhoff, Nicolas. "Old Models Can't Explain New Economy, Speaker Says." *EE Times*. 31 Oct. 2000. CMP Media, Inc. 25 Nov. 2000 <http://eetimes.com/story/OEG20001031S0022>.

Murph, Darren. "Internet2 Operators Set New Internet Speed Record." [Weblog Engadget] 25 Apr. 2007. Weblog, Inc. 17 Dec. 2007

<http://engadget.com/2007/04/25/internet2-operators-set-new-internet-speed-record/>.

"No Child Left Behind: A Desktop Reference." *ED.gov.* 14 Sept. 2007. U.S. Department of Education. 10 Apr. 2008 <http://ed.gov/admins/lead/account/nclbreference/>.

Papert, Seymour. *Mindstorms: Children, Computers, and Powerful Ideas.* New York: Basic Books, 1993.

Richardson, Caroline. "See No Evil: How Internet Filters Affect the Search for Online Health Information." *Kaiser Family Foundation.* 10 Dec. 2002. The Henry J. Kaiser Family Foundation. 15 Apr. 2008 <http://kff.org/ent-media/20021210a-index.cfm>.

Robinson, Sir Ken. "Do Schools Kill Creativity?" *TED: Ideas Worth Spreading.* 27 June 2006 <http://ted.com/index.php/talks/ken_robinson_says_schools_kill_creativity.html>.

Scorsese, Martin. "Scorsese's Acceptance Speech." *The Independents.* 16 Feb. 1996. 16 Apr. 2008 <http://godamongdirectors.com/scorsese/faq/scorsesespeech.html>.

Shachtman, Noah. "It's Teleportation—For Real." *WIRED Magazine.* 28 Sept. 2001. 11 Apr. 2008 <http://wired.com/science/discoveries/news/2001/09/47191>.

Sifry, David. "Oct 2004 State of the Blogosphere: Big Media vs. Blogs." [Weblog Sifry's Alerts] 14 Oct. 2004. Technorati, Inc. 17 Dec. 2007 <http://sifry.com/alerts/archives/000247.html>.

Sifry, David. "The State of the Live Web, April 2007." [Weblog Sifry's Alerts] 5 Apr. 2007. Technorati, Inc. 9 Sept. 2007 <http://sifry.com/alerts/archives/000493.html>.

Simpson, Carol. *Ethics in School Librarianship.* Worthington, OH: Linworth Publishing, Inc., 2003.

Sullivan, Danny. "Direct Navigation to Sites Rules, but Search Engines Remain Important." *Search Engine Watch.* 19 Feb. 2002. Jupitermedia Corporation. 7 Jan. 2003 <http://searchenginewatch.com/sereport/02/02-nav.html>.

Thibodeau, Patrick. "Computer Science Graduating Class of 2007 Smallest This Decade." *COMPUTERWORLD: Careers.* 5 Mar. 2008. 17 Apr. 2008 <http://computerworld.com/action/article.do?command=viewArticleBasic&articleId=9066659>.

"Top Sites." *Alexa: The Web Information Company.* 27 July 2008. Alexa Internet, Inc. 27 July 2008 <http://alexa.com/site/ds/top_sites?ts_mode=global?=none>.

"Top Sites by Country." *Alexa: The Web Information Company.* 25 July 2008. Alexa Internet, Inc. 25 July 2008 <http://alexa.com/site/ds/top_500>.

United States. Bureau of Labor Statistics. "Younger Boomers: 10.2 Jobs from Ages 18-38." 30 Aug. 2004. GPO. 30 July 2008 <http://bls.gov/opub/ted/2004/aug/wk5/art01.htm>.

Warlick, David. "10 Ways to Keep Your PLN from Running Amok!" [Weblog 2¢ Worth] 18 Mar. 2008. The Landmark Project. 8 Apr. 2008 <http://davidwarlick.com/2cents/archives/1394>.

Warlick, Ryann. Personal Interview. 13 Mar. 2003.

Wikipedia Contributors. "HyperCard." *Wikipedia*. 2008. Wikipedia, The Free Encyclopedia. 18 Mar. 2008 <http://en.wikipedia.org/wiki/Hypercard>.

Wikipedia Contributors. "The Three Rs." *Wikipedia*. 8 Aug. 2007 07:15 UTC. Wikipedia, The Free Encyclopedia. 5 Sept. 2007 <http://en.wikipedia.org/w/index.php?title=The_three_Rs&oldid=149930493>.

Wikipedia Contributors. "Wiki." *Wikipedia*. 2007. Wikipedia, The Free Encyclopedia. 9 Sept. 2007 <http://en.wikipedia.org/w/index.php?title=Wiki&oldid=156498459>.

Wilgoren, Jodi. "School Cheating Scandal Tests a Town's Values." *The New York Times*. 14 Feb. 2002. 21 Mar. 2008 <http://query.nytimes.com/gst/fullpage.html?res=9F06E1DE143FF937A257 51C0A9649C8B63>.

DATE DUE

Nov 6			
GAYLORD			PRINTED IN U.S.A.